Re
MW01241701

Once more love eludes Clella, now Catherine. Her marriage to a much younger man began as an adventure. What she thought was the love story for the ages is fraught with bitter disappointment, loneliness and betrayal. In *All That Matters*, the beautifully written sequel to *Pathways of the Heart,* Diane Yates tells, not only her mother's story, but her own as well. Catherine has taken up residence in my heart. Hers is a story I won't soon forget.

~~Rochelle Wisoff-Fields, author of *Please Say Kaddish for Me* and *From Silt and Ashes*

For Marilyn.
Blessings,
Diane
Prov. 3:5-6

All that Matters

By Diane Yates

DEER HAWK
PUBLICATIONS

Linda-1955

LouAnn-1955

Catherine and Diane-1956

Larry-1957

LouAnn and Diane-1957

LouAnn-1957

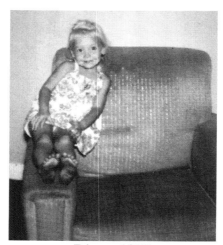

Diane-1957

Diane and Rick-1972

LouAnn, Catherine, Diane, Linda-1972

Rick, Catherine, Diane-1972

Catherine's Texas Family Gathering-1976

Diane-1976

Francis and Ginny-1976

Linda's Family-1977

Francis, Diane, April, Brian, Christa-1983

Catherine-1991

Catherine-1994

Francis and Diane-1995

**Francis Napping with Great Grandson,
Nick-2002**

Prologue
January 1997

*I go to prepare a place for you. And
if I go and prepare a place for you, I will
come
again and receive you unto myself,
that where I am, there you may be also.*
John 14:2b-3

The phone on the shelf of our
headboard rang. In a foggy haze, I answered
it. The familiar voice resonated clearly.

"I'm home now," Mother said, "here
in the mountains." Before I could speak, she
continued, "I just wanted you to know I'm
thinking about you."

I opened my eyes immediately. I
wished I was still asleep, and I desperately
ached to hear her voice again. She sounded
so real. Heat from my love resting next to
me usually kept me warm, but even so, I had
deep, cold chills and goosebumps covering
my body. I believe in dreams; not all of
them, but certainly some possess purpose
and meaning. In the darkness, I looked at the
clock as my mother's words echoed in my
head.

My husband, Rick, stirred and leaned
over me, resting on his elbow. "What is it?"

After I explained, he held me close
and stroked my hair.

"I miss Mother, the way she used to be, you know. I miss talking with her and telling her my troubles." I reached for the phone. "I have to check on her."

"It's four o'clock in the morning, Honey," he reasoned. "The nursing home would call if anything was wrong."

"You're probably right. I guess I can wait." Even though he made sense, I still felt uneasy.

Later that morning, the call came. "Yes, I'll meet the ambulance at the hospital," I told the nursing home. Driving my car above the speed limit on Highway 121, I sped toward Fort Worth and Plaza Medical Center. I remembered the last time I drove to see her at the hospital.

"Oh, it's you," she had said. "You always come." Tears silently rolled down my face as I signaled and changed lanes. I didn't bother to brush them away.

When I arrived, it wasn't like the last time. She lay there with her eyes open. I quickly moved to her side, hoping to provide comfort, but her vacant eyes didn't notice me. I took her hand in mine, but she didn't react. Even though life still coursed through her veins, she didn't appear to be there.

Mother had always been there for all of her seven children, wanting to remove their problems, working tirelessly to help in any way, and caring as only she could.

A nurse entered the room with an IV bag. "And you are?" she questioned me before assisting the doctor who was examining Mom.

"I'm Diane Yates, her daughter."

She hung the bag and connected it to the tube in Mother's arm. Another tube looped behind her ears and carried oxygen. The machine next to her bed made the sound of a heartbeat. I had scarcely absorbed the scene when that same machine erupted into a blaring alarm, startling me.

"Mrs. Yates, you'll have to wait outside," the doctor instructed.

Outside the room, I paced and searched for my cell phone in my purse. My hand trembled as I dialed my sister Linda; she and I shared in caring for Mom.

"Linda, it doesn't look good," I told her.

"I'll be there as soon as I can."

Then I called my oldest sister, Audrey, in Florida.

"Audrey, I think this is it." My voice broke. I told her about the dream, knowing she would understand. She and I shared the same mother but had different fathers. We also shared a bond stronger than blood—we both believed in the Risen Savior.

"I'll tell Mike and we'll make plans immediately," she told me. "You hang in there and call me if anything changes."

I continued pacing as I waited for an update on Mother's condition. Clella Catherine Burch's life had been quite a journey—from the Missouri Ozarks to the Gulf Stream waters, the mountains to the golden valleys. My sisters and brothers knew her as Clella, I knew her as Catherine.

Dad was thirteen and a half years younger, yet *he* always called *her* Kid. She once told me his reaction to the difference in their ages was, "It's not going to be a problem, Kid. When you grow old, I'll be there to push your wheelchair!" But, when the time came, I pushed it. I collapsed it, folded it, and lifted it into the trunk of my car only to reverse the action at whatever doctor's appointment she had that day. That was our routine for the last four years. She didn't remember my name, but she recognized the importance of our relationship.

Funny how things turn out. You think you know what's going to happen, yet it turns out that you don't. You live your life thinking you know what's important, but what if you're wrong? What if those things are not really what matters at all?

Chapter One
July 1957

"For I know the plans I have for you,
declares the Lord, plans to prosper you and
not to harm you, plans to give you a hope
and a future."
Jeremiah 29:11

After tossing his empty coffee cup into the sudsy dishwater, Catherine's husband, Francis, slipped his arms around her and gave her a lingering kiss. "I'm going to the office," he whispered.

She looked into his twinkling blue eyes. "Okay, I'll be there in a moment." She kissed him lightly again and then watched him walk away. His wavy brown hair and tall, slim form was made imperfect only by his right arm, which bent out and swung slightly wrong. It was a defect he bore since a horse crushed his elbow as a child. To her, however, he was perfect. He was the man she loved—the man who loved her.

The office, as it turned out, was only down the hall and to the right of the living room. A string of colored pennant flags waved in the wind and outlined the yard of their house on White Settlement Road, on the west side of Fort Worth. Several cars, and even some pickups, sat on display with the words "For Sale" written across their windshields.

Three years ago, she and Francis moved to Fort Worth when he took a job at Convair, an aerospace company with a promising future. Two years, one president, and a lost contract later found Francis on the layoff list because of lack of seniority. But, his ability to buy and sell cars prompted a wealthy investor to set him up in the used car business.

For forty-four-year-old Catherine, life had never been so good. Francis, her second husband, wanted her assistance in the office as well as when he purchased stock for the lot. She loved it. Catherine had married her first husband, Kenneth, at the age of sixteen. Back then, she went by Clella and was a farmer's wife during the Great Depression. She'd always been a keeper of the home, but this was the fifties. Now, she could work alongside the man she loved, figuring the books and running the office. Today, they were both going to retrieve cars he purchased earlier in the week.

Catherine followed Francis on Belknap Street. He and their lot man drove the newly-purchased cars while she drove theirs. Diane, their three-year-old daughter, stood next to her in the middle of the front seat. Belknap's busy traffic was slowed only occasionally by the red lights at the intersections. Cars weaved in and out of four lanes of traffic. The interchange ahead required lane changes and an exit toward Fort Worth proper. This always made Catherine a little nervous. What a contrast from the country roads in Wright County, Missouri!

She sadly remembered the day long ago when Kenneth taught her to drive and the fight that ended in him proposing. If he could only see her now—how far her driving skills had come!

Life had changed, but no matter who was at fault, the past could never be changed. A lump formed in her throat. She and Kenneth had six children who all still grieved the loss of their father. They probably always would. Francis had driven the three younger ones to school that morning. Nineteen-year-old Linda had left a few months before for a new job in California. The two oldest were both married and lived in Illinois. *Had they forgiven her, or had they simply decided love was easier than hate?*

At that moment, she realized Francis took the exit to the right and she missed the turn. Now, she was headed onward away from him. She panicked. "Oh, no! What do I do now?" Her eyes teared, but she blinked them away. She did the only thing she could think of: pulled off the road onto the shoulder. She looked across the grassy median and noticed Francis had parked his car on the side of the road and was walking the distance between them.

Little Diane put an arm around her and leaned in front of her face. "It's okay, Mommy. Daddy will save us."

Catherine gasped. "He will, won't he?" She laughed at the youngest of her seven children. Diane still had chubby little legs, blonde baby curls, dimples in her cheeks, and red lips as if she wore lipstick.

Catherine watched as Francis approached. She knew he would drive her through this maze and get the car back on the right road. He always came to her rescue. He loved her. *I can trust that, can't I?* Kenneth had been unfaithful, but Francis was different.

***** *

Summer 1957

Linda's hand shook as she signed the letter, "Love, Linda." It would take about two weeks to reach her mother. First, her letter, along with letters from the other girls, would be mailed to California where a priest would mail them all out so they'd have a California postmark, making the deception complete. It talked about California and about her wonderful new job. It was all a lie, so no one would know she had checked herself into a home for unwed mothers in Fort Worth.

A tear fell from her eye and onto the bottom corner of the plain, ruled paper. She quickly wiped it away, but the dampness left a crinkle on its surface. She sniffed and pulled a handkerchief from her pocket to dry her eyes. When she looked at the somewhat worn folded cloth with dainty stitched rosettes and mint green leaves, tears flowed freely. Her father had given her mother this handkerchief on her mother's sixteenth birthday. It reminded Linda just how different life was from how she thought it would be.

Her dad had been gone for three years, and she still grieved for him. Mother had given her this handkerchief as a token to remember him by.

Linda straightened, put her hand at her back for support, took a deep breath, and walked over to the lone window in her room. The Texas heat cast a brown hue on the grass, and the trees seemed dull and stagnant, as stagnant as her heart. She could see the Montgomery Ward's tower, Leonard's Department Store and downtown Fort Worth. How she longed to talk to her mother.

Linda ran her hand over her swollen stomach, then returned to the desk, folded the letter, and stuffed it in an envelope. She started to write the mailing address and immediately made a mistake. She addressed the letter to Clella Lathrom, but neither the first nor the last name belonged to her mother anymore. During a mid-life decision, her mother chose to go by her middle name, Catherine and she changed her last name forever when she remarried.

Frustrated, Linda jerked the contents out and tore up the envelope. She started over, addressing it to Catherine Burch at a location not even five miles away.

Over the past several weeks, Linda cried occasionally, but her resolve to accept responsibility for her pregnancy became her strength, her determination.

Fred's dark brown hair and boyishly good looks attracted her from the start. They had fun together, and she naively believed he loved her. She would never forget his reaction when she told him she was carrying his child, and she would never be so foolish about anything again.

She licked the new envelope and sealed it. When her baby entered the world, parents who desperately want a child would adopt it. She felt good about that, but found it provided little consolation for a broken heart and a life that would never be the same.

Up until that point, her life in Texas had seemed promising. She embraced the craze of the new rock 'n roll of the 50s and that heart throb, Elvis Presley. She enjoyed Fort Worth's Fat Stock Show and Rodeo tradition in January, especially those handsome Texas cowboys with their Stetsons. Everyone dressed western, and cowboy boots were a wardrobe necessity. School closed for a day so everyone could participate. She smiled as she remembered how she and her sister LouAnn rode horses in the parade last year.

Linda gave up her job in the personnel department of a local aerospace company, a position she felt fortunate to hold. A pregnancy out of wedlock would never be accepted, even in this fast changing world of 1957. It had taken all her fortitude to resign.

She missed her brothers and sisters, but she yearned for her mother most. She even missed her baby sister, Diane. On paydays, Linda often went shopping to buy Diane something special. She smiled thinking how the little one's eyes would light up at the latest baby doll or tea set.

In the beginning, Linda believed she would never be close to her mother's baby. No, any interaction would be uncomfortable if not altogether impossible. After all, Diane's father was Francis, and Francis was very much alive, sharing a life with her mother and siblings. Kenneth was Linda's real father. He wasn't supposed to be dead. He was supposed to still be married to her mother and either living happily on the family farm or in Peoria, Illinois. No, life wasn't what she thought it should be at all.

Linda still had two months of isolation left. Her unborn baby kicked a lot these days. She wondered if it was a boy or a girl. She wanted to be a mother, but not one without a husband. A permanent ache filled her heart. She would've been a great mom. She wouldn't make the same mistakes as her own mother, yet she wanted her mother now more than anything. She wanted to pour her heart out to the one who had lovingly raised her and desperately wanted Mom to make everything all right.

She sprawled out on her cot against the wall and stared at the ceiling. Tears silently continued flowing down her cheeks.

*****

Catherine rose early, before anyone else. It was a difficult habit to break that she acquired from early mornings on the farm with Kenneth. She opened the Folgers coffee, dumped the correct number of scoops into the metal basket in the pot, and placed the cover on top. She plugged the percolator into the socket and then looked out the kitchen window, waiting for the coffee to percolate against the little glass dome in the center of the lid. Dawn illuminated the back yard.

The rooster crowed inside the chicken coup behind the house. She and Francis raised chickens for fresh eggs in the mornings and, sometimes, fried chicken for dinner. The sounds reminded her of Missouri mornings, Kenneth, and most of all, her sister, Essie—whose farm hadn't been far from hers. She missed her Ozark Mountains, but she wouldn't trade her adventures with Francis for anything. In the last three years, she'd seen the cornfields of Nebraska, the plains of Kansas, the Indian reservations in Oklahoma, and the cowboys of Texas. These adventures made her feel younger than her forty-four years. They needed to since her husband was thirteen and a half years younger!

The coffee started percolating.

Life now had many conveniences, like indoor plumbing and automatic clothes washers, that most people in Fort Worth took for granted. She certainly didn't miss carrying water up from the spring or milking all those cows. Reminiscing, she thought about when she met Francis, how excited and free he made her feel. When she was at her lowest point, he picked her up, dusted her off, and loved her. Perhaps it wasn't right, but she lost the battle to resist. At first, Francis was an escape, a chance to laugh and dance and live again. Then, before she realized it, he'd become much more.

Her parents taught her the difference between right and wrong. Some of her family thought what she did was wrong, but was it? Yes, she was still married to Kenneth when she met Francis, but only on paper. Kenneth had deserted her. He deposited her and their four youngest children in Missouri, expecting her to live alone on a farm without running water. Meanwhile, he returned to Illinois to work and live in a modern world and forget about them.

Months passed and he never answered any of the letters she'd written. Catherine, determined to live in a home with water and electricity, moved her and the children into a newer house in Mountain Grove, a nearby town. Soon, her teenaged children became hard to handle. Buck, then thirteen years old, and Linda, sixteen years old, took up drinking and smoking. On more than one occasion, they were caught vandalizing neighbors' properties. Catherine needed the help of their father.

Her heart ached alone at night in her cold bed. She continued to write Kenneth, begging him to come home, but he didn't come. How could she have possibly known he still loved her? The day their divorce was granted, Kenneth grabbed her hand on the courthouse steps and pleaded with her to marry him again. She was almost persuaded, but the child growing inside her belonged to Francis—and her heart did, too.

Catherine asked God to forgive her when she read *I John 1:9*: "If we confess our sins, He is faithful and just to forgive us our sins and to cleanse us from all unrighteousness."

She knew He'd forgiven her, but had she forgiven herself? Would her past always haunt the present? Still, God gave her happiness and blessed her in many ways. Little Diane never knew a stranger and was such a precocious child. She took after her father. Catherine knew Francis couldn't be prouder. She made her choices and time went on.

"Good morning." Francis startled her as he slipped his arms around her and kissed her neck. "Coffee smells good."

She turned and hugged him, and they kissed tenderly. Then, she poured them each a cup and they sat down at the kitchen table.

"I was just thinking about Essie," she said. "Are you sure you want to do this? Go to the reunion, I mean?"

He took a sip from his cup. "If it's what you want, then I think we should go."

Catherine's family had planned a reunion at Essie and Jim's farm in Missouri. She took a drink and set her cup down. "Essie says she thinks everyone will be fine, that they all just want me to be there."

Francis touched her hand. "Are you up for it?"

Her siblings weren't used to seeing her with anyone other than Kenneth.

She sipped her coffee. "I don't know. It's the first time my family's come together since before my dad died." It would be difficult, but they were her family. She had to face them sometime. "I'd love to see everyone, though." She mentioned her siblings by name and added, "Audrey and

Alan will be there with Al and Van. Wallace will be there, too," she added. Wallace, her oldest, was bringing his wife, Donna, whom Catherine hadn't met. Fort Worth was about 900 miles from Peoria, Illinois, where Audrey and Wallace lived. She suddenly felt excited about the visit.

Francis stood and gathered some documents from the counter. "Then it's settled, we'll go." He sounded so sure of himself.

She hoped her family would welcome him, but expected it to be strained.

Catherine remembered the first time she met Francis's parents. They had objected to their son marrying someone older with children from another man. She'd been concerned, but all went smoothly. Diane captured their attention from the beginning as they both oohed and awed, counting her fingers and toes. Everything else just fell into place. Diane was their first granddaughter, and since Catherine was Diane's mother, they automatically accepted her. Perhaps they felt their son was finally settling down.

Francis drained his cup. "What time does Linda's train get in?"

"Two thirty this afternoon."

"I should be able to get away. I can probably drive you to the train station," he offered.

"Great!" She'd gladly let him do the driving. "I'm excited and can hardly wait. I knew she wouldn't like California for long."

"What's not to like?" Francis protested. "I love it out there. It's comfortable all year round—none of this awful heat in the summer or ice in the winter."

"I meant it's so far away!" She smiled and envied Francis. Until she married him, she hadn't been anywhere but Missouri and Illinois. His previous truck-driving years allowed him to see much of the country including California.

He laughed and his eyes teased her, "You wouldn't like it, though—lots of traffic, freeways, and fast driving!" He kissed her. "I'm going to shower and head over to River Oaks. I need to see a guy about a car."

*****

At 2:15, Catherine, Francis, and Diane walked inside the station to meet Linda's train. Glass, marble, and brass adorned the walls and floors of the twelve-story Texas & Pacific Building on W. Lancaster Street. Catherine had been here before, but its beauty always astounded her.

Francis looked at the huge marquis above them. "I don't see her train listed on the board." People bustled about the crowded train depot.

Catherine strained to read all the train schedules when a familiar face caught her attention. Surprised, she exclaimed, "Oh look, she's here already!" Catherine expected to wait on Linda. She immediately ran to her daughter and hugged her tight. "I'm so glad you're here. I missed you so much."

"I missed you, too, Mother."

Mother's intuition noticed something in Linda's voice. Catherine took a long look at her daughter. Her beautiful, thick auburn hair shone as it curved over her shoulders, but something was different. Her shapely, slender figure had gained a little weight through the middle, and her small bust appeared fuller.

"How was your trip, dear?" Catherine asked. A mist appeared in Linda's eyes, confirming Catherine's suspicions. She didn't know what, but something happened.

Diane tugged at the hem of Linda's dress. "Linda, Linda, Linda," she repeated until she got her sister's attention.

Linda bent down and hugged her. "Oh, I missed you so much!"

"Did you bring me anything from Cafornia?"

Linda laughed. Catherine was glad Linda loved her baby sister and always spoiled her by buying her things.

"I have something in my bag. We'll see what it is when we get home."

"Ah!" Diane sighed in disappointment.

To Catherine's surprise, Linda turned to greet Francis and gave him a quick hug. It wasn't necessarily unusual behavior, but Catherine believed Linda was avoiding her scrutiny. Something was wrong; she knew it.

"Did you pick up any good looking boys on the train?" Francis teased as he took her suitcase and they all headed for the car.

*****

That evening after dinner, Francis began strumming his guitar. "Buck, you got your harmonica?"

Buck pulled the juice harp out of his pocket. "Sure do."

Everyone gathered in the living room to listen to the music. LouAnn sang. Catherine enjoyed having her children together, but Linda suddenly rose and fled the room. Catherine followed her and found her crying on the bed.

"What is it, Honey?" she asked, stroking her hair. "What's wrong? I know something's wrong." When Linda kept crying and didn't respond, Catherine tried again, "Tell me. You can tell me."

A long time passed before Linda spoke through sobs, "I wish I could tell you, Mother." She rolled over and Catherine looked at her tear-stained face and troubled eyes.

"Oh, Honey. It can't be that bad. Is it something that happened in California?"

Catherine waited patiently. She expected her daughter to start talking any minute and didn't rush her. "Are you worried about not having a job? Don't, because you can stay here until you find something."

Linda's tears started again and she shook her head. "No, no, no, Mother. It's something I have to deal with by myself."

Yes, that was Linda—always trying to be the strong one, too proud to admit she needed anything. Then suddenly, Linda sat up and grabbed her mother. "Oh, Mom, it hurts so much. I don't think I'll ever…" her words trailed off.

"What hurts? What is it?"

Finally, Linda admitted, "I wasn't in California, Mother."

"What do you mean you weren't in California? You wrote me often."

"I was at…I was at a home for…a home for unwed mothers."

"What?" Catherine heard the surprise in her own shrill exclamation.

Linda started crying again. She nodded her head. "I gave birth to a little girl, here in Fort Worth."

"What do you mean?" Catherine struggled to comprehend. "Where is she?"

"She's gone. Adopted. I miss her so much. I feel awful."

"Adopted?" Catherine couldn't believe it.

Linda nodded and continued, "I thought I was doing the right thing. I thought no one needed to know. But I know, Mom, and I wish I hadn't done it. For nine months she was my constant companion. Now I need her, but she's gone."

Catherine stiffened. "What do you mean she's gone?"

"I signed the papers. There's nothing I can do."

"Well, we'll just see about that!" Catherine retorted with determination. "First thing tomorrow morning, we're going down there and getting her back!"

*****

Linda lay in her bed, anxious and hopeful. *Was it true? Her mother had always been able to do almost anything. Could Mother really make all this right? Could she possibly hold her baby girl in her arms as early as tomorrow?* How she longed to do just that.

*****

Catherine didn't sleep at all. Instead, she thought about Linda and the past several months. She remembered Linda screaming, "I hate you." That was four years ago—after Buck had discovered her and Francis alone. Since then, she believed her daughter had forgiven her, even thought they had grown closer. Catherine was proud of Linda and their relationship. But now, she began to think perhaps Linda hadn't forgiven and forgotten. *Why would Linda have decided to endure a pregnancy alone without confiding in me?* Tears rolled down the sides of her face and dampened her hair and pillow. How alone Linda must have felt. Catherine's heart broke for her daughter and the granddaughter she hadn't seen.

She knew Linda still struggled to accept Francis. Though Linda didn't know it, when Catherine told him about the adoption, he'd been just as intent on getting the baby back as herself. He even wanted to go with them to the home. Catherine welcomed his support. She kept going over the details of what she might do tomorrow. She must convince the home to give the baby back. If not? Well, she couldn't fail, she just couldn't.

*****

The next morning, the three of them sat across the desk from the administrator of the home, a portly woman dressed in a white blouse and black skirt. Her short black hair, over-curled from a permanent, framed her face. White-rimmed glasses curved up to a point on either side of her eyes. She never smiled. Instead, she kept her nose elevated slightly as she defied every argument Francis, Catherine, and Linda made.

"She thought it over and she's changed her mind," Catherine said. "That baby belongs to Linda and she wants her back."

"No, Mrs. Burch," the woman countered. "Linda was over eighteen when she signed the paperwork. The baby is not hers."

"That's a piece of paper." Catherine shouted. "We're talking about a baby, a little life that belongs in our family."

"The baby is already with the adoptive parents."

"We'll get a lawyer and fight this," Francis threatened.

"You can, but that's going to be expensive and everything we've done is legal and binding." Her eyes narrowed and she leaned forward slightly. "You don't have a case," she hissed.

Unfortunately, a few hours later, a lawyer confirmed what the lady said. They could fight it, but it would cost more than Francis and Catherine could afford and, in the end, they would probably lose. This devastated the three of them. They all quietly returned home.

How Catherine had wanted to help, but she had no control over the legal system. She felt heartbroken.

Chapter Two
1958

Francis guided the car around the curves and over the hills of Route 66. He kept the speedometer at seventy, staying alert thanks to the snoring from the others in the car. Only headlights from an occasional oncoming car peeked through the darkness. The road wasn't difficult until after the Ozark hills.

While everyone slept, he had time to think. The lights from the dash illuminated his little girl, stretched out on her mother's lap in the front seat. She was a part of him. His folks always fussed over her, which pleased him immensely. For once, something endeared him to his parents. He glanced at Catherine who rested peacefully. He loved her, but life had changed from that time when they first met. Back then, they enjoyed each other in exciting newness outside the normal routine.

He slowed and made the turn onto Highway 60 in Springfield without the change of speed or the whine of the transmission waking his passengers. He hoped Catherine's family reunion would go well, but he had his doubts. He had to admit that the thought made him nervous. He already knew her sister, Mag, from the tavern she and her husband, Ed, owned in Mountain Grove. They had introduced him to Catherine in the first place. Essie and Jim had come to his parents' home once when he and Catherine were visiting. They seemed cordial enough and thrilled to see Diane, who was only a baby at the time. But there were still many family members left to meet.

Even though Catherine and her first husband were separated when he met her, Francis knew the family hadn't taken well to her divorce and remarriage. He assumed that some blamed him for messing around with a married woman. One month before Diane's birth, Catherine's first husband, Kenneth, tragically died. Catherine changed when she received news of his death.

The rising sun illuminated the countryside through the car windows. In the rearview mirror, Francis noticed LouAnn stir, yawn, and sit up straighter in the back seat of their '54 Plymouth. She looked out the window before realizing Larry's leg rested on top of hers. "Get off me," she yelled and pushed him.

"Hey," Francis whispered, "let's not do that." But, it was too late. The commotion had awakened not only Larry, but Buck and Linda, too.

Catherine straightened and glanced around. "Look, kids, we're in Mansfield. It won't be long now."

She rubbed Francis's shoulder and yawned. "You must be tired. You want me to drive awhile?"

"No, I'm alright." He'd rather drive than ride. "But, is there any more coffee in that thermos?"

"Francis, you drove all night!" Buck exclaimed.

"Yeah, when I get behind the wheel, I don't like to stop for much." Catherine's children called him Francis. He didn't mind. He knew he could never be like a father to them. He liked Buck with his bubbly personality and mischievousness. LouAnn was smart, too smart for her own good sometimes. Larry had grown so much in the last three years, it was hard to remember the little boy he'd been. They all liked rock'n'roll, which Francis hated. Regardless, Buck and Larry would play harmonica to his guitar.

"I've got to go to the bathroom," LouAnn announced.

"Me, too," Larry said, yawning.

Francis chuckled. "I'll pull over on the side of the road up ahead. You can go as nature intended!" Finding a filling station with a restroom was rare in these parts, and finding one open at this hour was impossible. "Or you can wait and use the outhouse in Mountain Grove." Most of the country had updated to indoor plumbing, but in rural mid-America there were still many businesses and homes without that luxury.

Francis turned on the radio and started punching the pre-set buttons, looking for a station with good music. Elvis Presley's voice blared, rocking the radio with "Heartbreak Hotel." Francis quickly punched another button.

"Ah, turn it back. We liked that one."

Diane opened her eyelids and Francis asked her, "What are we supposed to listen to?"

She reacted promptly, knowing the answer. "Honky-Tonk music!" she shouted. Then she quickly added, "But, I liked that one."

Now, he had a riot on his hands. To end it, he pulled over for a potty break. When everybody got back in the car, Ernest Tubbs sang on the radio and that was that!

*****

Catherine loved her Missouri Ozarks. For most of her life, this was home—the rolling hills, oak and walnut trees, cherry and apple blossoms, cool spring mornings, and snow-covered winters. Now, the end of June, the mild weather contrasted with the stifling heat in Texas. She always loved coming back. Anticipation rose within her, but something else also—a pang that started at her core and nagged away at her joy.

She was born here, married, loved, and raised six children here. Her mother and father were buried in these mountains. Essie and Jim's farm was located about ten miles to the north of Highway 60. She couldn't wait to see her sister tomorrow at the reunion, but today, they would go to Francis's folks' house. He had driven all night, stopping only twenty minutes or so to close his eyes.

She felt a little queasy at the thought of tomorrow. She wanted to see her family but worried about this particular reunion and her family's reaction to her new husband. No matter how her life marched ahead, memories followed her. Some were haunting, others cherished.

She glanced at Francis, who was driving and tickling Diane at the same time. Yes, her husband was younger, but he loved her. His desire for her in their bedroom melted any difference in their years. At least their life together was just that—together. He hadn't left her to go pursue his dreams. Surely, he would always love her. He seemed content to manage a car lot with a wife and her three children as well as their own little one. He certainly loved his little girl.

Francis's parents lived on Main Street. Even though his mother, Anna, worked hard at the shoe factory, she always immaculately cleaned their small home. This morning, Catherine was confident that Anna would have breakfast ready when they got there. Francis's dad, Everett, would have already been to their farm and milked the cows. How she loved drinking fresh cow's milk. This was only *one* of the things she missed about the country.

The car continued up and down hills and around the winding curves. Ahead on the right was where she told Francis she was pregnant with Diane. Catherine could scarcely believe that life could change so dramatically in only three and a half years.

It seemed like an eternity ago when she and Kenneth started their life on the farm. When Kenneth held their firstborn son, Wallace, in his arms, she was convinced they'd never be apart. That moment would forever belong to her and Kenneth. But, they each had made of their lives what they wanted. Kenneth pursued drinking, gambling, and women. She turned to the guitar player who showed her affection. The pathways of their hearts led different directions.

She couldn't wait to see Wallace and Donna tomorrow at Essie's. On the farm, she had depended upon him. Many times, it was just the two of them ensuring the chores were done. They took care of the farm through blizzards and heat waves. She could always rely on him. Wallace was the one who told her about his father's lady friend.

Catherine was confident she would have his support, but when she and Kenneth separated, Wallace was furious with her. He seemed to have a double standard. In his heart, his father remained blameless, even though he witnessed everything. At the time, she felt hurt and betrayed by her son.

*****

The next day, Francis drove slowly down the gravel road off Highway 38, past the one-room Robinett Schoolhouse, and to the end of Jim and Essie's driveway. He parked behind a '52 Chrysler. The sun shone and there wasn't a cloud in the sky. He saw children sliding down the cellar and forty to fifty adults standing or sitting in chairs on the lawn. This must be the whole gang. Linda, Buck, Larry, and LouAnn, who had been making all kinds of noise in the back seat, now bounded out of the car and ran to see their cousins, aunts, and uncles.

Francis walked to Catherine's side of the car and opened her door. She smiled up at him and took his hand. Their gazes steadied on each other.

"Stick with me, Kid," he told her.

"And you by me," she replied, half laughing. They hadn't gotten far when Essie, Jim, and several of her relatives came to greet them. Francis remained tense through the normal introductions. He finally started to relax when he noticed Mag and Ed. The two of them, along with Dude, Wallace, and

Alan, all had beers in their hands. *This might not be so bad after all,* he thought.

There was the usual fried chicken, potato salad, and watermelon one would expect to find at a family reunion, but the Garners didn't stop there. He'd never seen so many different dishes.

To his surprise, he enjoyed talking with Essie, Jim, Verbie, and George. Catherine's family was intelligent and stimulating. Jim not only talked about current news and politics, but also hunting and aerospace advances.

Some of the family drank excessively, others not a drop. Some, like Dude and Wallace, strived to treat him cordially. He enjoyed hearing the old stories, and Kenneth was mentioned only occasionally, which wasn't so bad.

In the brightness of the day, each of the families assembled for pictures to record the event. All-in-all, Catherine's family was great. He'd have to get used to them calling her Clella, though. He knew that was her name, but she had always been Catherine to him.

He watched as she laughed and talked with her family. She seemed truly happy. But one thing surprised him, she laughed a little too much and sometimes, her conversation seemed forced, as if she was overcompensating for some insecurity. *Why should she feel insecure?* He had never known anyone more capable of doing anything than her.

*****

The next day, Catherine sat between Francis and Diane in the pew of the Burch's little country church. A summer breeze blew through the windows as birds sang in the trees. Everett Burch led the congregation in singing hymns. Catherine enjoyed the singing and the service, especially when Francis played the guitar for his parents as they sang.

At the end of the service, a slender young lady with long dark hair played "Just as I Am" on the piano. Catherine noticed Francis couldn't keep his eyes off her. That night, she decided to mention it.

As he climbed into bed beside her, she said, "She was very pretty."

"Who was?"

"The piano player you kept staring at."

He started laughing as he pulled her into his arms. "Are you jealous? I really wasn't looking at her. I watched her play the piano, that's all." She thought about his answer. Knowing he loved music, Catherine understood him observing the piano player. He kissed her and they rested between the sheets of the Burch's guest bed. Tomorrow, they'd all drive back to Texas.

Chapter Three
1959

Sixteen-year-old LouAnn sat close to Roger as he cruised down River Oaks Blvd in his '57 black and white Ford. A warmth swept through her as he put his arm around her on the back of the seat. His Stetson almost touched the roof of the car. He always wore his cowboy boots, and tonight was no exception. He had taken her to a drive-in movie. Now, the last thing on tonight's agenda before that goodnight kiss was dragging down the main strip. All the high school kids did it.

Roger was definitely a cowboy and not a dragster, but he did have a nice car. Linda had introduced them, and then Roger taught LouAnn how to ride horses.

She laid her head on his shoulder. Right then, she heard it, or did she imagine it—the throaty rumble of a finely-tuned hot rod. It was a sound so familiar, her heart skipped a beat. She lifted her head to look in the rear-view mirror. LouAnn saw a set of headlights approaching them at record speed. As the car closed the distance between them, neither it nor its driver could be mistaken. *Oh, no,* she thought. She wanted to shrink into the floorboard, but mostly, she worried about Roger handling the situation. Inside, she trembled.

The light in front of them turned red, and both cars came to a stop. The red and white '55 Chevy and its 283 small-block engine, four-speed corvette transmission rumbled beside them. Billy revved the engine. LouAnn stole a glance at him, but Billy looked directly at Roger, who returned the stare.

"Let's go, cowboy," Billy goaded. "Let's see what you got under that hood." The light turned green, engines roared, rubber squealed and smoked, but no car could beat Billy Nettleton's '55 Chevy. In fact, he raced it every weekend and had never lost. LouAnn knew this because she'd been the girl sitting next to him on many of those occasions.

LouAnn was attracted to Billy from the start and dated him off and on for the last few months. He could make her laugh, but his stubbornness and quick-temper clashed with hers. They often fought with fury.

Billy and the Chevy disappeared from view as it made a sudden right turn.

"I'm sorry about that," LouAnn said.

"Don't worry about it. I knew I couldn't beat him, but I couldn't turn down a dare."

"Billy has a way of getting under your skin. Trust me, I know." She turned and looked out the window briefly, not wanting to look him in the eye.

Roger parked on the street outside her house and turned the engine off. In the dark, stars twinkled and crickets chirped. "I had a great time," LouAnn said, even though the earlier encounter with Billy still unnerved her.

Roger slipped his arm around her, pulling her closer. "Me, too," he said before kissing her. LouAnn felt the strength in his arms. His embrace made her feel safe. This tall, dark, and handsome cowboy let his soft lips linger tenderly. Roger was perfect in many ways: always kind, considerate, and thoughtful. LouAnn wanted more than anything to love him. When he released her, she looked into his wanton eyes, desiring to feel the same passion, but something was missing.

A light shone into the back window and she could hear the sound of that '55 Chevy. It stopped right behind them. After a rev of the engine, Billy turned the motor off and jumped out of the car.

With deliberate strides and desperation in his voice, he yelled, "LouAnn, what are you doing? Get out of the car."

Roger jumped out and came around to her door. Ignoring Billy, he pushed his way in front of him and opened the door for his date, acting as a shield between Billy and LouAnn.

Billy leaned around him to look at her. "Is this what you want? Is he what you want?"

"Don't do this, Billy. Not now," LouAnn begged. But, she knew she couldn't dissuade his hot-headedness when he got riled. Billy didn't stand as tall as Roger. In some ways, his character was exactly opposite of Roger's. His reddish brown hair matched his fiery personality, but when LouAnn looked into his blue eyes, she saw the yearning there—the same as hers. She realized that what had been missing with Roger was what she felt with Billy.

Roger turned on him, "Hey, let me see her home, okay?"

Billy ignored him. "LouAnn, either you tell him tonight you're with me, or it's over between us." He paced and stomped wildly.

LouAnn heard Billy's words, but the tone of his voice told her he meant it. She looked at Roger. She saw the love in his pleading eyes. Panic struck and everything spun around her. She couldn't bear to break anyone's heart. LouAnn looked back at Billy and recognized his determination. If only she could run inside and find refuge.

"I mean it, LouAnn," Billy said.

She loved Billy. She even loved his fiery temper. She could no longer deny it. Even though he was being rude, she loved the fact he stood there, declaring his love for her.

Roger's dismay showed as LouAnn stood silently. "LouAnn?" he pleaded softly.

She took a deep breath. "Roger," she began, glancing at him only briefly before staring at the ground. It took great resolve to lift her eyes to meet his again. "Roger...I'm sorry." She watched his eyes close. When he finally opened them, she saw his disappointment and heartache. "Roger, please. I'm so, so sorry. I didn't mean to hurt you."

He didn't say anything and didn't look at Billy. Instead, he straightened the hat on his head and turned. He got into his car and drove away. She watched his Ford come to a stop at the intersection down the street. It stayed there and she could see his silhouette in the streetlight. He stared in his rearview mirror for a few minutes before he hung his head. Her heart broke for him.

Billy's voice ended the silence, "I knew you'd come to your senses." He touched her shoulder, but she spun around to face him.

"Billy, how could you do that?" LouAnn's anger burned.

"How could I do what? LouAnn, I love you. What did you expect me to do? Were you going to keep seeing us both? 'Cause if so, I'm movin' on." His arms fell to his sides, and he shifted his weight from one foot to the other. She knew he needed to hear from her how she felt.

She had a strong desire to fall into his arms and kiss his lips. "Billy," she shook her head. "I love you. I guess I always have. But, why can't you ever think about me and my feelings?" She turned to walk inside.

Billy chuckled. "Well, heck, I thought I was," he called out as he ran to stop her.

*****

Catherine watched the whole scene from the dark little window in the hallway upstairs. At such a young age, she knew her daughter had faced a difficult decision tonight. She now wished she had intervened. She saw Billy clasp LouAnn into his embrace. They kissed passionately.

*****

Summer 1959

Again Catherine stood up and looked out the window. It was almost midnight and still no sign of Francis. This wasn't necessarily unusual behavior; he often went to the club downtown to hear the headlining group. He especially liked Bob Wills, a regular there. Catherine didn't mind too much. She couldn't always go because she needed to stay with Diane, but Francis needed to be around music. However, recently, he seemed nervous and edgy. Catherine knew something wasn't right with him and couldn't help but worry.

Tonight, LouAnn went out with Billy. Lately, Linda spent all of her time with her new beau, Norman Johnson, a Fort Worth Police officer who was a sweetheart with a friendly personality, dimples, and baby blue eyes. He doted on Linda. Both of her girls were in love and not very interested in babysitting their little sister. Before falling asleep, Catherine said a prayer for her husband and children. She prayed often, but never felt worthy of receiving an answer. Going to church only became a reality whenever they visited Francis's parents in Missouri.

In the heat of the next afternoon, her husband finally came home. He sat on the divan and stared blankly at Diane, who played with her dolls in the middle of the living room floor. Catherine watched as he rubbed his fist along his chin. His contorted face and shaking hands frightened her.

"Would you like a cup of coffee?" she asked without asking him where he'd been. He nodded but didn't look at her. When she returned, she set a cup in front of him on the coffee table. "Diane, Honey," she said softly, "take your dolls into your room and play." She watched her husband anxiously.

Francis picked up his cup only to let it slip and spill coffee onto his pants and floor. He jumped slightly and yelled a curse word.

"Francis, what is it? What's wrong?" She sat down next to him, but he abruptly rose and walked to the window. Staring out at apparently nothing, he rubbed the back of his neck.

"Francis?"

Still, he uttered no response. Catherine began trembling. Something was terribly wrong.

"I'm no good for you," he said in a hushed tone. Pointing down the hall toward Diane's door, he continued, "And I'm no good for her, either."

"What are you talking about?" Catherine wasn't sure she wanted an answer. She imagined the worst. He hadn't come home all night. Could he be seeing someone else? After all she had been through with Kenneth, she didn't think she could bear that. In the beginning, she believed she and Kenneth had a forever love, but over the years, his affairs and gambling came between them. Surely, it wasn't happening all over again. She had an impulse to run out of the room and not seek any further explanation, but Francis broke the silence.

"It's not good." He stared at her now. In his face, she saw sadness, desperation, and… something else. "I don't know what to do," he admitted. That's when she recognized the fear in his voice.

"What are you saying?" *Please don't say it*, she thought. *Don't tell me you're in love with someone else.* She backed up slightly.

Francis sat back down on the divan and shook his head. "I have to get you and Diane out of here. It's not safe." He wasn't making any sense. The thought of her leaving him sounded a lot like the separation Kenneth had suggested all those years ago. Kenneth had left her to go work in Oregon. When he returned, things were never the same between them. She tried to ignore it, but after twenty-five years of marriage, he abandoned her and the children.

"Why?" she whispered. Was he trying to get rid of her, just like Kenneth had done? *No, God, please no.*

Francis rubbed his hands together nervously. "Leo isn't going to be happy." Leo was the man who owned the car lot. "I thought I could win it back, you know? But, before I knew it, the night went bad and I lost it all!"

Catherine couldn't believe what she heard. *Had he been gambling?* She thought he went to the club to hear music like the other times.

"What are you telling me?" she asked. "All of it?" She didn't need to ask the amount because she had prepared the deposit the day before.

He nodded and rubbed his chin with his fist again.

"You lost nine thousand dollars?" She heard the hysteria in her own voice.

"Yes. I don't know what I'm going to do. You and Diane need to leave. It could get dangerous around here."

"Dangerous? Francis, you're talking crazy. We'll just tell him and make arrangements to pay it back." Her mind raced, seeking solutions to the problem.

"You don't make arrangements with someone like Leo and his two thugs."

"Thugs?" *What was he saying?* "You mean his associates?"

She sensed he would have laughed had he not been so frightened. "Honey, those guys aren't 'associates.' They're not even bodyguards. They make sure people like me don't take Leo's money."

They spent the next hour trying to solve the problem. Thinking of idea after idea and then why each wouldn't work, they exhausted all their options. Somehow, that money needed to be replaced. But how? There was no one from whom they could borrow that much money. Francis insisted that telling Leo and offering to repay was unthinkable. Catherine wondered why he hadn't thought of that when he used the money in the first place. Then she got an idea. It wasn't what she preferred, but she'd never seen Francis so worried.

Finally, she suggested, "Okay, here's what we're going to do," she said, kissing him on the cheek. "You're going to leave and take Diane to your parents. I'm going to stay here and pack the things we need to take with us. I figure we can float some of the money. We can hold off on reporting the payments that come in until later. The deposit won't really show up missing until three or four weeks from now."

"I can't leave you here," he said. "These guys don't play around."

"I'll be fine. What would they do to a woman? Besides, I can always call Norm. And Larry's here with me."

"It might work," he said, thinking. "I could take this evening's train and be home by tomorrow night."

She added to his thoughts, trying to sound convincing. "When you get back, we'll take the next couple of weeks to finish up before leaving."

"We can leave in the night," he agreed. "We'll go back to Mountain Grove."

She watched the lines of worry across his forehead decrease. She reached for him, they kissed, and he clutched her tighter than ever before. Mountain Grove was where they had started. In many ways, it was home.

Yes, this situation wasn't one she would have chosen, but somehow her heart soared. Francis, who was thirteen and a half years younger, hadn't fallen in love with someone else at all. He needed her. She had to help him get out of this mess.

*****

I watched in the mirror as Mom brushed out the curls in my long, blonde hair. Mom tied the bow in the back of my blue cotton dress. I wore white anklets with lace and my black patent-leather shoes tapped as I walked. At five, I placed my hand in Daddy's and kissed Mom goodbye. I was going to see Grandma and Grandpa. I couldn't have been more excited.

Daddy and I climbed aboard the Missouri, Kansas, and Texas railroad car number nine and took a seat in the middle. He squeezed my hand before moving to the ticklish place just above my knee. I squirmed, giggled, then looked up and smiled at him. We were having fun. The train made a swishing sound and started moving slowly. Gradually, it gained speed and started rocking in time with a clickety-clackety rhythm as it left Fort Worth.

We ate dinner in the diner car and then returned to our seats. I began reading Larry's *Fun with Dick and Jane* book. Larry taught me to read about a year ago. He taught me one paragraph. I memorized it and then matched words with the rest of the written words. I eventually caught on to the sounds certain letters made, and the rest was easy. I loved reading.

As the sun set, the light dimmed to the faint glow of the small lamps on the walls. I yawned and could hardly hold my eyes open. Daddy let me lay my head on his leg. I fell asleep and didn't wake until the train arrived in Mountain Grove. Since I was still really sleepy, Daddy carried me.

When he left to go back to Texas, I didn't cry. I loved Grandma and Grandpa. During the next month, whenever my grandmother worked at the shoe factory, I stayed at Aunt Sarie's across the street. She wasn't really my aunt, just a close family friend. She read exciting stories to me every day from the Bible. Aunt Sarie made stuffed animals and dolls. I loved to play with the monkeys she made out of socks and the Raggedy Ann dolls that were unlike any I had ever seen. I would turn them upside down, the dress would reverse, and they would become a different doll.

That month, I attended Vacation Bible School, and some days I went with my grandpa as he did chores like plowing, milking, and mowing. Every Sunday, we attended church. Grandma fried chicken and cooked garden fresh green beans. A *Peace* I wasn't familiar with lived in their house. I didn't question why I had come to stay with my grandparents. I only knew that one day soon, Mommy and Daddy were coming for me.

*****

Catherine and Francis worked overtime to execute their plan. Meanwhile, sixteen-year-old LouAnn and Billy decided they wanted to marry. Catherine didn't have the energy to argue. She finally gave in and signed the papers to allow their marriage. Although sometimes his temper got the better of him, she believed Billy was a fine young man. They were both young, but they did seem to love each other. After all, Catherine herself first married at the age of sixteen. With LouAnn's maturity, surely they would be okay.

Catherine's children were all growing up. Linda and Norm made plans to marry and move to Washington State. Buck, who was in the Army, would be getting out soon and also planned to go to Washington. Catherine secretly packed and prepared for Francis, Larry, and her to leave when the time was right. She missed Diane.

During the days, Catherine and Francis worked on the car lot, selling cars and collecting payments on existing car loans. This allowed them to accumulate cash, concealing their loss until a final accounting. Each passing day, Catherine's nerves tensed, and it became harder to sleep. She knew Leo could pay them a surprise visit anytime. She hoped the missing money wouldn't be evident until they were long gone.

In the heavy heat of an August afternoon, Catherine watched as a familiar Chevy drove on the lot. LouAnn got out. Catherine saw her daughter's moist swollen eyes.

"What is it, Honey? What's wrong?"

LouAnn started crying. "I have to go with you, Mom. I can't live with Billy. It's never going to work."

Catherine talked with her at length. She felt confident LouAnn and Billy just had a normal fight like many newlyweds. However, LouAnn was only ten years old when Catherine's marriage to Kenneth ended. Her children, who were angry with her at the time, wanted to stay with their father. She left them to start a life with Francis. Catherine believed LouAnn still struggled with feelings of abandonment. As recently as last year, LouAnn still had nightmares. If LouAnn wanted to go with them to Missouri, Catherine couldn't leave her again. Francis, Catherine, Larry, and LouAnn would travel by night.

Tomorrow, she and Francis would take the remaining cars to auction and sell them. With a little creative bookwork, they would make a tidy deposit into Leo's account and prepare for him a final accounting of their business. Hopefully, they'd be long gone before being discovered.

She wasn't sure how they'd make it with so little money, but somehow they would.

Chapter Four

In the back bedroom, I opened my eyes to the morning sun. I smelled bacon and heard voices.

"How do you want your eggs, LouAnn?" Grandma asked.

LouAnn? Then I heard Mother's voice and Dad chimed in, too. I threw off the covers and ran for the kitchen. Four long weeks passed since I saw them last. I pushed open the door. Dad, Mom, Larry, LouAnn, and Grandpa sat at the table as Grandma placed bacon, toast, and jam in front of them.

"Mommy," I yelled as I ran to her, hugged her tightly, and climbed on her lap. "LouAnn, I didn't know you were coming."

"Yep!" My sister kissed my head.

"Where's Billy? Did he come, too?" LouAnn glanced at Mom.

"No, Honey, he didn't come." I thought she might cry. I turned to Mom, expecting her to explain, but she said nothing. However, as they all talked I gathered that LouAnn and Billy had split up. This made me sad.

In the afternoon, while Mommy and Daddy napped and I played with my doll, a red and white '55 Chevy rumbled in the street and parked in front of my grandparents' house. I watched as Billy slowly walked up the sidewalk, stepped on the porch, and approached the front door. The house shook as LouAnn ran to meet him. They talked, but I couldn't hear what they said. Soon, Billy kissed her and they made up. The sparkle gleam returned to her eyes and her face beamed. They loved each other, just like Grandma and Grandpa, Mommy and Daddy, and Linda and Norm. Everything was going to be all right. LouAnn would return to Texas with Billy where she belonged.

A few days later, Dad, Mom, Larry and I settled into a little house in town. They called it a Cracker Jack box. It was so small that Larry and I didn't have a bedroom, but we didn't mind. We slept on pallets in the living room. Dad drove a truck and delivered car batteries all over southern Missouri. I noticed Mom didn't cook Dad's favorite, which was steak, for dinner anymore, thank God. I hated it! Now, she mostly cooked yummy beans and cornbread or delicious chicken and dumplings. Mom was a great cook. Sometimes, the electricity wouldn't work until Dad paid the bill and she would have to cook on the gas stove by candlelight.

Larry and a friend built a go-kart. I just knew if I asked him sweetly enough, that he'd let me drive it, but he never did.

Instead, he took me for rides, and that was pretty fun, too.

It snowed in December right before Christmas; it was the first time I'd seen snow! We made a snowman complete with buttons, which Mom gave us, and an old hat of Grandpa's. We played in the white powdery dampness and threw snowballs.

Buck and his wife, Virginia, came for the holidays, but Linda and Norm couldn't come because they were expecting their first baby in January. I hadn't seen Buck since before he got married. When he drove his two-tone, two-door '56 Pontiac into the driveway on Christmas Eve, the excitement started. He ran around the car to open the door for Virginia. She was beautiful—tall and slender with green eyes and light brown hair. He grinned from ear to ear as he hugged Mother.

"Hi, Mommy," he said, laughing teasingly. He stood tall and proudly as he introduced Virginia to us.

Even though our house was small, Mom said it had elastic walls. She and Dad pulled the mattress off their bed. Buck and Virginia slept on the mattress, Dad and Mom on the box springs. As Daddy, Buck, and Larry played music, we all sang and laughed. Larry and I fell asleep on Christmas Eve in front of the Christmas tree. Shiny glass ornaments, silver tinsel, and brightly-colored lights made it the most beautiful tree ever.

I loved Christmas; even if we didn't get many presents, it was still my favorite time of all. Mom made Christmas fun, but I think Dad enjoyed it more than any of the other adults. Larry and I hung our stockings above the fireplace, but when we awoke, they had multiplied. Stockings hung there for all of us, regardless of age, filled with our favorite things: fruit, candy, other little trinkets for Larry and me, and a carton of cigarettes for the older ones.

Laughter filled our tiny home as we gathered around our kitchen table for Christmas dinner. Smiles lit up the faces around me and I realized the joy of family.

*****

1961

Since moving back to Missouri, Francis and Catherine had no telephone. When they fled Texas, they poured all their funds into replacing as much of Leo's money as possible, leaving themselves very little resources and certainly nothing with which to pay "Ma Bell." Catherine missed being able to talk with her older children. She waited anxiously for the postman each day, anticipating letters from across the miles.

Catherine noticed a light shining through the window and moving across the room. She parted her homemade curtains to see Essie's blue Ford parking outside. She folded the letter she just read, which had been sent "air mail, special delivery," and placed it back into the envelope. Stuffing it under some papers on the kitchen table, she wiped the tears away from her face with the back of her hands and hurried to answer the door. She was always excited to see her sister, but she wouldn't share the contents of Audrey's letter with Essie today. First, she would take time to digest the heart-wrenching news, herself.

Essie knocked at the door while Catherine ran her fingers through her hair in front of the mirror and dabbed at her red eyes with a handkerchief. Then, she opened the door. Essie's eyes met hers, and Catherine hugged her. "I'm so glad you've come," she said. "Want some coffee?"

Essie reached out and grabbed her arm. "You've been crying. You heard from Audrey, didn't you?"

Catherine searched Essie's eyes. *Did she know already? Yes, she knew.* Audrey's world was collapsing, her heart shattered, and somehow Essie knew before Catherine. Catherine cherished her oldest daughter with all her heart; she had rocked and soothed her as a child, but Audrey had already confided in Essie, and Catherine had to wait to read a letter. Catherine and Essie both blinked away tears.

"Yes, I just got her letter." Essie hugged her again while Catherine desperately tried to understand why Audrey turned to Essie for comfort first and not her. Of course, Audrey would call her aunt because Essie had a phone, not to mention that Essie had been like a second mother to Audrey over the years. Nevertheless, it still hurt.

"Oh, Clella, what are we going to do?" Essie's voice broke on the last word. She took a deep breath before continuing. "I talked to Genevieve and she said she doesn't know what's gotten into her son. She said she hopes he comes to his senses soon."

"Genevieve always really liked Audrey," Catherine said about her daughter's mother-in-law. She and Essie settled into two chairs at the kitchen table. Shaking her head, Catherine added, "I knew it wasn't a good idea for Audrey and Alan to work different schedules. With Alan working nights and Audrey working days, it's just not good for a young couple, I tell you."

"Well, you're probably right. I still can't believe it. Jim and I thought she and Alan were a match made in heaven."

"So she called you. How is she? How did she sound?"

"Oh, Clella, she sounds lost." Essie placed her hand over Catherine's.

"Who is this woman? Do I know her?" Catherine asked.

"No, she never told me. She said it didn't matter who she was."

"Little Al and Van, bless their hearts," Catherine sighed. She suddenly felt a heavy weight. When she and Kenneth had gone their separate ways, Essie and Jim probably uttered a similar statement about her own children. *That was different wasn't it? Kenneth had abandoned her. She didn't mean to fall in love with Francis.*

Catherine stood and stared out the kitchen window. Her mind returned to another kitchen when she and Audrey quarreled over her love for Francis. "Audrey," she had said, "your father just lost interest and now, it's too late. You don't know; this could happen to you and Alan one day." She remembered Audrey's face, how her eyes squinted and her lips narrowed. "This will *never* happen to Alan and me," she had spewed. Catherine wanted to hug her daughter then and help her to understand. Now, she again wished she could hold her, tell her how much she loved her, and assure her that everything would be okay.

Essie shook her head and filled their cups. "It's always hardest for the children," she said.

Catherine searched Essie's face. Though she feared she might find it, there was no condemnation there. Instead, she found the same love and compassion the two of them had always shared. "Yes," Catherine agreed, "it is." She knew that the decision Alan made, just like the decision she had made, would forever change the lives of everyone involved, especially the children.

When her sister left that afternoon, Catherine wrapped her arms around her. "Essie," she said, "I want to thank you for being there for Audrey." She continued because she needed to say more. "You've always been there for my kids and it's meant a lot."

Essie had a gleam in her eye. "I haven't done anything you wouldn't have done if the shoe were on the other foot."

As Catherine watched her sister drive away, she thought about her life. So much had changed since she and Essie attended the dance in Mansfield with Kenneth Lathrom and Jim Robinett. She had fallen completely in love with Kenneth. She couldn't have possibly conceived how life would end up for them—divorced after twenty-five years and Kenneth dead soon thereafter. Just like when Audrey married Alan, she never dreamed it might end up like this. *We're often so certain of what we need, of what we think is important, that we lose sight of all that really matters.*

Catherine anxiously waited for Francis to come home. She longed to hug him tightly and tell him how much she loved him. Life wasn't easy, by any means, but her love for him remained strong. They would always be together, wouldn't they? She could trust his love for her, couldn't she?

Chapter Five
1961

Packing their possessions required fewer boxes this time. Catherine gingerly wrapped the set of Currier and Ives dishes and placed them in a box. She found a safe place amid the dishcloths for her mother's pink eyelet bowl of Depression glass. It was a wonder it had survived the moves she and Francis made from Missouri to Kansas, to Texas, and back to Missouri.

The depressed economy of the little town of Mountain Grove left Francis unemployed. Soon, they wouldn't be able to pay the rent, much less keep the utilities on. Of course, there were no guarantees anything would be different anywhere else. President John F. Kennedy took office last January, and the couple had high hopes in him.

Francis and his Uncle Dallas walked through the front door. The two of them had grown close years earlier when they were both truck drivers. Dallas and his wife, Marie, had three girls and lived in Kansas City, where Francis now decided he and Catherine should move so he could look for work to get them back on their feet. They sold their car to have money on hand and intended to rely on public bus transportation. Larry left to go stay with LouAnn in Texas.

"Can I get you two a cup of coffee?" Catherine asked from the kitchen. "I have a couple of cups I haven't packed yet." She began pouring even before they answered. Soon, the boxes were all loaded in Dallas's car.

"Mommy, can Trina sit in the car with me?" Diane's favorite doll, Trina, went everywhere Diane did.

"That's fine dear." Catherine directed six-year-old Diane to sit next to her in the back seat of the car. Francis sat in the front seat and talked with Dallas.

"Awe, this is awful," Francis told him, "but I think Kennedy will get the aviation contracts moving again. That's all I need. Since I got laid off from Convair, there's just been nothing. No one's hiring."

"Well, I sure hope he can get folks working again," Dallas added.

"So, you think I'll be able to find something in Kansas City?"

Catherine listened to her husband talk as the car once again took her away from Mountain Grove. They drove around the square, passing all the familiar places: Ben Franklin's dime store, Richard Brother's Grocery Store, Sam's drugstore, and the gazebo in the middle of town.

She remembered that gazebo and all the Saturdays when she, Kenneth, and their children visited with their friends. The kids ran and laughed and musicians serenaded them all with melodic Ozark tunes. She smiled as she thought of little Buck flirting with the ladies, Audrey hanging out with her friends, and Wallace walking with his girl. She resurrected a vision of Kenneth, tipping his hat and uttering "how do" to those he met. All the ladies would swoon if he tipped it in their direction. It felt like a lifetime away, and in a sense it was—an old life in which she used to live.

They passed the shoe store where seven years ago she had run into Francis as she shopped and they secretly planned their next rendezvous. Pain struck her heart as the car rolled on beyond the stop sign and in front of Barber Funeral Home. She attended many funerals there, paying respects to friends and family alike. Not only had she gone there to find little Larry after a car hit him, but also on that fateful day when she went to tell her husband of twenty-five-years goodbye. She had touched his still hand, and her heart broke for their children who had lost their father.

Francis winked at her and reached for her fingers, giving them a gentle squeeze. She knew he was telling her it would be okay. Even though they had fallen on hard times, he remained determined to find a way. She trusted him, even in the face of so much uncertainty. Diane laid her head in Catherine's lap and slept for most of the trip.

One week later, Catherine unpacked the last box of dishes, stacking them in the old cabinets that still didn't feel clean even though she had scrubbed and scoured them twice. The second story apartment of an older house in downtown Kansas City didn't require much rent, and the bus stopped just around the corner. Catherine felt the responsibility of making each place a home, no matter how humble. Besides, Diane liked playing with the little girl in the downstairs apartment.

Francis left earlier to look for a job. Catherine knew things were critical. She took a small piece of ham and added it to the beans she soaked earlier. She had just enough cornmeal to whip up a small pan of cornbread. Not his favorite, but it was food.

She heard the door open and saw Francis walk in with a key in his hand, smiling from ear to ear.

"What?" Catherine couldn't help the excitement in her voice. "Did you find something? What's the key for?"

He put his arms around her. "Well, it's not much, but I do have wheels!"

"Daddy, Daddy," Diane tugged on his pants, "did you find a job?"

He turned and picked her up, "Yep, and you're really going to like it."

"What? What is it?"

"Well, I'm going to drive an ice cream truck and sell ice cream treats to little kids just like you." He shrugged at Catherine. She knew any work was better than none.

Diane jumped up and down. "Can I have an ice cream, too?"

"We'll have to see. We can't have you eating up all the profits!" Francis tickled her.

Later that evening, Francis told Catherine, "This is only temporary. I've sent my application into Boeing. They have jobs in Seattle."

"Seattle?" Her eyes widened and her jaw dropped. This was news to Catherine, who hadn't even contemplated moving so far away so quickly. "You think you have a chance?"

"I don't know why not. It's the same work I did in Texas. We'll just have to wait and see, I guess."

"But what about Boeing in Wichita? You've worked there before and it's closer."

He shook his head. "The contract is with the plant in Seattle. It's prettier out there anyway."

With their daughter asleep on the sofa in the other room, she welcomed his embrace as he pulled her into his arms. His hands explored the sensitive areas of her body, igniting the fire within her. Oh, how she loved him.

That night, she couldn't sleep. She and Francis might actually rebound from the financial depression they'd experienced since leaving Texas. She had never been west, but Kenneth often talked of its beauty. Imagine, she might be going to Seattle, Washington, home to the World's Fair next year. What would Essie say? Ten years ago, Catherine would never have believed this would be her life today.

*****

August 1961, Kansas City

I thought Mom was going to squeeze the life out of my fingers as she pulled me up the steps of the city bus. She tugged me in the direction of the first empty seats. When we sat, the heat surrounded me like a suffocating closet. The windows were open, but a breeze scarcely entered. When it did, I couldn't help but smell the sweaty fat man sitting across the aisle from us. I glanced briefly; I didn't want Mommy to accuse me of staring. His bushy eyebrows and uneven moustache both glistened with drops of sweat that had rolled down from his forehead, and his shirt had large wet spots under his arms.

The bus stopped to pick up more passengers—colored people with three kids about my age, one boy and two girls. I don't know why they walked past the open seats, but they did. I turned around and watched them as they kept walking and finally sat in the seats at the very back of the bus. Mom touched my hand and told me to turn around. I always did what Mommy said, especially after the other day when I asked to go play with Jane. She said no, but I went anyway. She came after me with a switch and used it on my legs all the way home. No, from now on I'm going to listen to Mommy!

At the store, I saw all kinds of things I wanted. "Can I have some M&Ms?"

She smiled at me and then sighed. "No." She picked up a can of potted meat, a loaf of bread, a small package of beef tips, some grapes, and some tomatoes.

"Can I have an ice cream bar?"

"No, Honey, this is all I have money for." I was disappointed, but when she touched my cheek, I knew she loved me. As we returned home on the hot, stinky bus, I couldn't keep from frowning.

"Maybe Daddy will have some ice cream for you on his truck," Mom suggested.

With a newfound hope, I sat up a little straighter.

When Daddy walked through the door that evening, he carried a treat just for me.

"Put it in the freezer until after dinner," Mommy told him. He kissed her and said the beef stew smelled good. It did. I was anxious to eat so I could have dessert.

He poked his finger in my belly. "You ready to start school next week, Gizmo?"

"I'll say! I've been waiting for a lifetime to go to school." He laughed. Last year, Mommy had tried to talk the school into letting me start even though my birthday wasn't until September 25. "You don't think they'll tell me I can't go again this year, do you?"

"No, Honey," she answered. "This year, they have to let you go."

That next week, the day after Labor Day, I sat in a classroom for the first time. I thought it was the greatest thing ever! I barely got settled into the routine when, after only four weeks, Daddy came home with the news. He seemed really happy, but I wasn't so sure.

*****

Catherine stretched out on the couch in the living room, enjoying the evening breeze blowing through the open windows of their apartment. Cars honked and a police siren blared. Suddenly, the front door opened. Francis hurried in and announced, "Boeing needs me to be in Seattle by October 5."

Even though she could see the excitement in her husband's face, she struggled with the words the minute he spoke them.

"Diane," she said, "why don't you get your nightgown on and go to bed? You have school tomorrow."

When they were alone, she asked, "How are we going to get to Seattle?"

"Well, I'll have to go first. Then you and Diane can join me. We'll figure it out."

This was what she'd feared. Francis would leave her for work on the west coast. *When and if we reunite, will he have changed just like Kenneth did? Will what happened to me and Kenneth happen to me and Francis?* She didn't want to risk that now, but his eyes sparkled with hope and his face beamed with excitement. How could she possibly say anything disappointing to him?

Still, they were virtually stranded in Kansas City. For the last four weeks, she'd walked Diane to and from school while Francis drove an ice cream truck for what little earnings he could muster. Now, with the summer over, his job would be, too. She bought groceries sparingly, and they did without many things just to make ends meet. *Although Boeing in Seattle presents a great opportunity, how will we get from here to there? Will I be forever left behind?*

"But how will you get there?" she reasoned. "You don't have a car and we don't have money for bus or train fare."

"I'll hitchhike." He said casually as if it should be obvious to her.

"Francis, that's a long way. I'll be worried sick."

As he pulled her into his arms, she watched his eyes roam about their two-room apartment. "This is our chance, Kid, to get out of here. Trust me, it'll be okay. Truckers always pick up hitchhikers, and I get along just fine with truckers." He laughed and his blue eyes danced.

He kissed her tenderly, stirring up passions—passions she couldn't ignore, nor did she want to. She felt the warmth spreading through her body. She ran her fingers through his curly locks above his forehead. His hands caressed her curves and she quickly responded, matching his desire. His embrace felt heavenly.

*****

Francis worked a full week at Boeing. On Saturday night, he rode the city bus to downtown Seattle. Then, he walked and took in the sights. The whole town buzzed, preparing for the 1962 World's Fair, whose theme revolved around science and space. Amidst the construction, he could see the tall, stick-like structure with a saucer shape on top. They called it the Space Needle.

He stopped in a little bar and ordered a beer, even struck up some conversations. Talking to complete strangers never bothered him. What *did* bother him right now, even more than he wanted to admit, was this overwhelming desire to see his wife and daughter. He had to leave Catherine and Diane with Uncle Dallas. Diane had to change schools, making this the second one for her first year.

Working in aerospace again felt good. Francis had been trained for this type of work. It was a far cry from driving that ice cream truck! With his first paycheck, he started saving to buy train fares for his wife and daughter. After being married for seven years, he didn't know he could miss someone so much. He wanted to see seven-year-old Diane and hear all about school. He'd been alone long enough and couldn't wait until they could all be together here in Seattle.

He rented a little track home, one of several in a row facing another row with a little bit of grass separating them. It was another Cracker Jack box, but was all he could afford. Next Friday, when he got paid, he'd go to the train station and purchase the tickets, then send for them. In the meantime, he'd go home and reread the letter Catherine sent, maybe even write her one tonight and put it in the mailbox on Monday.

*****

After a month with Dallas and Marie, Buck came and took Catherine and Diane to Illinois until Francis could send for them. Catherine and Diane spent some days with Buck and his family, but mostly they stayed with Audrey. Audrey had recently married a young man named Mike. At first, it seemed strange seeing Audrey with him, but Catherine could tell he was a good man. She was happy her daughter found love again. She had feared that Audrey would never forgive her, but during this stay, the two of them reestablished that special bond between mother and daughter.

Audrey's sons, Al and Van, were slightly older than Diane, but the three of them got along splendidly. The boys had early-American twin beds in their room— the kind with the half wagon wheel at the head and foot. Playing Cowboys and Indians, they enjoyed pretending those beds were covered wagons, especially after watching *Wagon Train* on television.

Yesterday, the mail brought another letter from Francis. Her heart leapt with joy when she found train tickets for her and Diane. "I'm tired of being away from you," he wrote. "Please come as soon as you can." He signed it, "I love you and miss you both." She pressed the letter against her chest. Even though she was almost fourteen years older than him, Francis really loved her. Things hadn't changed between them like they had with Kenneth. Instead, Francis wrote often and couldn't wait for her and Diane to join him. She and Francis had been through a lot in their seven short years, but how thankful she was to have found another love, surely a stronger love.

Even at forty-nine years old, she felt young and alive. She could hardly believe it, but soon, she'd be on a train with her seven-year-old daughter heading out west, a land she'd only dreamed about. Their future together couldn't be brighter, could it?

Chapter Six

The loud speaker wasn't audible as Catherine entered the crowded train depot. People hurried, running in all directions as if they would miss their train. Surveying the scene, Catherine realized how much the world had changed since she'd been born. Large cities had sprung up over much of the nation, paved roads led everywhere, and fast cars were the fashion of the day. Young people had become careless and disrespectful. Boys dressed in cuffed jeans. They rolled up their t-shirt sleeves and stashed a few self-made cigarettes, or sometimes even a whole store bought pack, in the rolls. Girls didn't always wear dresses. Some wore capris or even shorter shorts.

Catherine hated saying goodbye. She hugged her oldest daughter and spoke through tears. "Thanks, Honey, for everything. I don't know what I would've done without you."

"Oh, Mother," Audrey said, her voice choking as they hugged again. "Write and let me know you made it okay."

Dressed in overalls and a matching cap, the conductor cried out, "All aboard." Catherine blotted her eyes with a handkerchief. Two thousand miles was a long way and she didn't know when she'd see

Audrey again, but at least they'd rejuvenated their relationship. She would always cherish the memories of the farm and Audrey helping her with the milking, canning, and taking care of four younger children. But, that was life before, and now, she must forge ahead. Taking Diane's hand, she boarded the train.

After they found their seats, Catherine watched Diane make her doll, Trina, some space beside her. Later, they would walk to the diner car to have some lunch.

The next morning, Catherine took Diane up the stairs to the observation deck. This car was covered with a dome of glass. As the train forged on in its clackety rhythm, Catherine beheld a land of hills and dark trees stretching out as far as the eye could see. A few hours later, a big sky hung over prairie land, and snow-covered mountains capped the view in the distance. The beauty of this vast land was breathtaking.

Altogether, the trip from Illinois to Seattle took three days and was exhausting. Diane behaved well and kept herself busy when she wasn't staring out the window at the scenery. Catherine couldn't wait to see Francis. As the wheels kept turning on steel tracks, the locomotive approached its destination. What a sight she must be! She needed to shower and fix her hair, but before the train pulled into the station, the most she could manage was a clean face and fresh lipstick. She searched the crowd for her husband, but didn't see him. As the train slowly came to a stop, she noticed a familiar shape, standing alone and dangerously close to the tracks. His weight rested on his left side and his right arm hung at a slightly awkward angle. Their eyes met through the window and she smiled.

"There's Daddy," she told Diane.

"Daddy!" Diane started waving. Catherine gathered their things. A man walking down the aisle stopped to let them out.

"Thank you."

When Catherine reached the steps of the train, she saw him waiting for them. He hugged her and they kissed briefly. Then he picked Diane up and started teasing her. Catherine's world felt right again as the three of them walked to the car. Everything she held dear, all that mattered in her life, revolved around this man. Being in the state of Washington with Francis excited her. He hadn't left her. Instead, he'd made sure they joined him as soon as possible.

*****

1961

On my first day of school in Seattle, the secretary escorted me to my class. I trembled as I entered the room filled with first-grade strangers, all of whom turned to stare. That didn't bother me nearly as badly as what the teacher did next. Without showing me to a seat, she yelled across the room and told me to go somewhere and get something for the art project the class was currently working on. I struggled to understand her confusing instructions. *What does she want me to do? Where does she want me to go?* When I couldn't figure it out fast enough, to my complete horror, she came from behind and with her hand swatted my bottom in front of everyone! I wasn't one to cry, but it would take several months to overcome this embarrassment.

As I walked to and from school each day, I passed a small church with stained glass windows and a steeple. "Could we go this Sunday, Mom?" I asked one evening.

She hesitated and then smiled. "You know, I think it would be okay if you wanted to go to Sunday school by yourself," she answered. "It's just around the corner."

"Really? By myself?" The prospect of having this freedom thrilled me. It didn't even matter that I might not know anyone there. I just wanted to go.

That Sunday, I attended the little church. The sweet Sunday school teacher explained that I could win a Bible for memorizing the *23rd Psalm*. I didn't have a Bible, so I wanted to memorize that chapter of *Psalms* more than anything. Mother helped me, and after I did, I couldn't have been prouder of my Bible.

Larry, who had been in Texas with LouAnn, soon joined us. I had been walking to school alone, but now he and his friends walked with me.

"I can't wait until Santa comes," I told them.

One of Larry's friends started laughing. "Santa?" He laughed some more. "Hey, guys, the little one here believes in Santa!"

"Leave her alone, Tommy," Larry said sternly.

"What are you talking about?" I questioned.

Tommy approached me, but Larry pushed him. "She's too old to believe in Santa. You're her brother. You tell her."

Larry didn't say anything, but Tommy continued, "There is no Santa Claus."

"Is too!" I argued and looked at Larry.

"It's your parents, Stupid. They fill your stocking when you're asleep." The boys made several comments about it being silly to think a fat man in a red suit actually flew in a sleigh around the world delivering toys.

This revelation devastated me. Then something even worse happened: I accidentally found my Christmas presents before they'd been wrapped. I realized that the fun of receiving gifts was not knowing what they were before I opened them. For example, I already knew the square flat one was a *Tom & Jerry* book. I loved to read and I loved *Tom & Jerry*, but it sure was hard pretending to be surprised.

A young girl who lived in one of the little houses facing ours got a bike without training wheels for Christmas. Her father taught her how to ride. I longingly watched the two of them. When he noticed me staring, I flinched, backed up, and started to leave.

"Would you like to ride?" I heard him ask.

I looked around to see who he was talking to. Realizing it was me, I answered, "I don't know how."

"Come and I'll teach you." Patiently, he taught me, too. I thought riding was the greatest thing ever. His daughter graciously shared her bike. I knew exactly what to ask Santa to bring me next year. *Oh wait, I forgot, there is no Santa Claus!*

*****

Francis whistled as he placed the last of the tackle in his box and prepared the fishing poles. He had rented a cabin in the mountains by the river and looked forward to fishing with Larry. He loaded the luggage and fishing supplies in the trunk of the car. Catherine brought him the bags of kitchen staples. Soon, the four of them drove along the highway on their way to a fun-filled weekend. It had been a long time since they'd been able to relax and enjoy a few of life's simple pleasures.

When they reached their cabin in the woods, picturesque evergreens, flowing streams, and green banks surrounded the furnished lodge. Catherine walked inside. "Oh, this is beautiful!" Her approval pleased Francis. "Look at this kitchen!" she marveled. "It's huge!" It had a long, curved bar and six stools. There was also a table and chairs in the dining area.

He placed his hand on fifteen-year-old Larry's shoulder. "We'll have to gather wood for the fireplace."

"I'm on it," Larry replied. "I noticed plenty of fallen branches outside. I'd be more worried about us starving if we don't catch anything!"

Francis laughed. "Oh, that's not a problem, least ways not for me. I'm not sure about you, though!" he teased.

"Oh, yeah? We'll see about that."

Later that evening, they relaxed in front of a cozy fire while Catherine cooked their fresh catches. Both he and Larry caught a fair share.

"You want to see my paper dolls, Daddy?" Diane asked him.

"Paper dolls? I thought you forgot to bring your toys." He tickled her above the knee.

"I did," she giggled. "Mom gave me some cardboard. I drew them myself and cut them out."

He looked at the boy and girl paper dolls she had made. Then Diane showed him the clothes she made for them out of tablet paper.

He glanced at Catherine who was cooking fish. "Did you help her with these?"

"Nope. She did them all by herself."

"That's really good, Gizmo!" and he tickled her again.

Francis decided to take a look at the fish frying. As he snuck up from behind and put his arms around her, she jumped. He felt the curves of her bosom before she readjusted his hands.

She nodded toward the fireplace. "The children," she laughed quietly.

He kissed her neck. "Later, then," he whispered.

Life was good. After a day in the green woods with fish beckoning from the clear streams, he enjoyed relaxing and watching Diane pester her brother. Larry was fifteen and she was seven, just perfect for being a nuisance.

Chapter Seven
June 1962

The semi-truck barreled past the little Fiat parked on the side of the highway, lifting and rocking it. Catherine feared the wind might actually turn them over. The windows rattled and the whole car shook from side to side, waking Larry and Diane in the back seat. Catherine quickly raised her finger to her lips, motioning for them to remain quiet as Francis slept for a few minutes. She wasn't sure which would be worse, for the car to turn over or for Francis to wake up before getting some much-needed rest.

They had driven through Idaho, Utah, Wyoming, and Colorado. There, they spent the night with Lois and Wayne, Francis's sister and her husband, before resuming their trip to New Orleans and completing their now seventh move in eight years.

Catherine enjoyed their travels and considered it all adventurous as she marveled at the mountains, prairies, streams and deserts along the way. It was all so beautiful and diverse, sometimes very different, from the Ozarks where she had grown up.

Francis had transferred from Boeing's Seattle plant to the New Orleans facility. He would be working on the Saturn V rocket for NASA. Even though the beauty of Washington took her breath away, the rain and cloudy weather dampened her spirits. She couldn't wait to see this warm place known for its jazz and Mardi Gras.

When the next big rig passed, the force of the wind awakened Francis. After a thermos cup of coffee, he was ready to resume this almost three-thousand-mile journey.

After several hours and crossing a few more borders, Diane asked, "How much farther?"

"Sshh, let's not ask that question again," Catherine suggested.

Francis answered, "We're not far now. We should be there by late afternoon, I'd say." He winked at Catherine before adding, "We've made pretty good time."

The little car followed the two-lane highway. Cypress trees dripping with moss lined the roads through the bayous of the Cajun state of Louisiana. All the windows were rolled up to take advantage of the air conditioning in the heat.

Randomly, Diane asked, "What's a parish?"

"Why do you ask?" Catherine questioned her.

"That sign said Benton Parish, population 3,205."

Francis explained. "Most states are divided into counties. In Louisiana, those are known as parishes."

"Why is that?" This time it was Larry who was curious.

"Well, I believe it's because of the French and Roman Catholic influences in the area."

Finally, at about 2 p.m., they crossed a small bridge with green-covered water on both sides and then turned into the driveway of a massive two-story white house. Towering oak trees shaded the luscious, neatly-trimmed green lawn, which had to be at least ten acres.

"Look at this!" Catherine exclaimed, taking in the sight of their new home. There was a large front porch, and from the side she could see a glimpse of the screened back patio. Just then, a woman stepped out of the shadows.

"That must be Mrs. Landry. You kids stay in the car," Francis ordered. "Your mother and I will only be a minute or so." He got out and went around the car to open the door for Catherine.

Mrs. Landry's dark, weathered face could hardly be seen beneath the netting attached to her hat. A scarf draped down from its brim and covered her neck before tying in front. Every other part of her body was covered with clothing. Even gloves covered her hands. "Are you the Burches?"

"That's right. You must be Mrs. Landry. I'm Francis. This is my wife, Catherine."

Catherine smiled and offered her hand to the older woman. "How nice it is to meet you, and how good it is to be out of that car!"

"I suppose ya'll are pretty tired. Come, I'll show you the house."

Catherine felt something bite and glanced down at her arms. She squealed and squirmed as mosquitos covered her skin.

Mrs. Landry cast her a glowering look. "Yes, you'll need to cover up well. There are always mosquitos." She turned and led them into the house. Catherine's uneasiness relaxed as Francis reached out and clasped her hand in his.

"Now, Mr. Burch, I think I told you that I live in a small apartment around back. You'll be renting the main house. All the furniture stays, and I'll expect you to take good care of it. My boy mows the yard, so you won't have to worry about that." She removed her hat and began giving them the tour of the Southern-style home. "So you work at Boeing?"

"Yes, I start next Monday."

"Fine, fine. It's a good company. A lot of people around here work there." She left them to tour the upstairs.

"What do you think?" Francis asked Catherine when they were alone.

"It's just beautiful." She never said a word about the mosquitos; this was his moment. He'd chosen the house from ads and contacted Mrs. Landry, making all the arrangements from Seattle. He never ceased to amaze her.

Francis called her over to look at the view from the bay window of the master bedroom. Grasping her hand, he pulled her into his arms and held her close. As if she was a teenager, her breath caught. His eyes sparkled. "What do you think, Kid?" Excitement washed over her with an undeniable heat and she knew he felt it, too. His lips met hers.

From the doorway, Mrs. Landry cleared her throat. "I trust you find the house to your liking."

Catherine pulled away flushed, but smiling. Without losing eye contact with her husband, she replied "It's just perfect, Mrs. Landry, exactly as you described."

Their few belongings arrived the next day and they spent the rest of the week getting settled. Francis and Larry went fishing at the bayou and met the owner of the bait shop, Bert, who offered to let them use his pirogue, a Cajun style canoe.

Diane loved her room, which also had a bay window. She placed all her baby dolls on its ledge. Larry wanted the attic bedroom upstairs with its sharply-angled ceiling. It faced the back of the house. He could lie on his bed, look out the window, and watch the trains on the railroad tracks in the far distance. Catherine believed they would all be happy here.

*****

1962

The afternoon summer sun was slipping lower in the sky when Catherine realized she hadn't heard or seen Diane since lunchtime. "Diane," she called, entering her daughter's room. The dolls on the shelf hadn't been moved, all the toys were in place, and the bed was undisturbed. *Maybe she's outside playing.*

Catherine walked out the patio door and searched the yard. No sign of her seven-year-old. She looked toward the shop, which housed the barrels that Diane often liked to run on like a lumberjack on a log. The barrels hadn't been touched.

She cupped her hands around her mouth. "Diane!" she yelled. "Diane!" She looked for any sign of movement. Nothing. She wished Larry was here, but he went fishing right after lunch, and she didn't expect him back until supper. *Where could she be?*

Railroad tracks ran along the back of the property, but she was sure Diane wouldn't venture that direction. Catherine glanced toward the highway in front. The huge oak tree shaded the driveway. She ran to the front yard—not there. Down the road, cypress trees covered in moss draped over the bridge at the bayou. Catherine's breaths became shorter and faster as panic seized her heart. Diane couldn't swim.

*****

The dock swayed as I stepped on it. I grabbed Larry's hand. Trees grew in the water. We couldn't see the sun or the sky because of all the growth and hanging Spanish moss. I stared at the water, at least I think it was water; it actually looked like a thick, green film of slime and grit.

Larry untied the canoe. "Come on."

I tried to pull my hand out of his. "Don't forget I can't swim."

"I'll keep you safe. After all, what are big brothers for?"

"Um…you sure it's okay for us to take the canoe?" I stalled.

"Oh, yeah, Bert told me I can use it anytime I want. And it's not a canoe; they call it a pirogue down here. Now come on."

Larry stepped in first, and sure enough, that green, slimy stuff moved in the water. I took a deep breath and trusted my brother. As I climbed in and sat down, the boat rocked. Larry started paddling from side to side. Several seconds passed before I began breathing again. He smiled at me and made small talk, trying to make me feel better. I couldn't help staring at the green film and wondering what I would do if I accidentally fell in.

I just started to relax when he warned, "Keep your eye out for alligators." I hadn't seen an alligator, but I knew they lived in the bayou. Larry took the trap he brought with us, placed the bait inside, and dropped it in the water. "I'm going to catch us a mess of crawfish. If I get enough, we'll have 'em for dinner."

I wrinkled up my nosed. "I'm not eating 'em. Yuk!" He showed me a crawfish the other day and it reminded me of an oversized bug, a creepy crawly thing.

I relaxed more and more as the pirogue glided through the water. Crickets chirped, frogs croaked, and even some birds sang. Then, I heard a sound I didn't recognize.

"What was that?"

"An owl."

Larry knew everything, which I thought was pretty amazing considering he was only eight years older. He pointed to a branch high up with a strange looking clump of feathers perched there. As I stared, its head rotated forward from the back. I jumped when it opened its eyes and screeched. These mesmerizing sounds of the bayou created an adventure unlike any I'd known.

Larry sniffed and turned his head from back and forth. "You smell that?"

I inhaled. Yes, I could smell something. "Yeah, it's sweet—almost like root beer. What is it?"

"Over there." Larry started paddling faster toward the shore and a tree with strange leafy blossoms. "Yep, that's a sassafras tree. We're going to take back some roots so Mom can make us some sassafras tea."

I never had sassafras tea. He dug his knife out of his pocket and carved out some roots. They looked like mere pieces of wood to me, but they did smell sweet. He handed me a rag. "Here, wrap them up in that."

As he climbed back in the boat, I shuddered as a snake slithered its way down the bank and into the water. Even though a fog-like mist settled in around us, streaks of light proved it was still daytime. Nonetheless, we'd been gone a long time. I hoped Larry could remember how to get back, because I sure didn't.

"Shouldn't we head home?" It was a question, but I meant it as a direction.

He winked and turned the boat around. "Yeah, we need to check our trap." When he reached the spot, he pulled the basket out of the water. It was full of crawly, pointy, bugged-eyed, creepy creatures, clasping onto wire and dangling all over.

"Eww!" I squealed. "You can't put those things in this boat!"

"We got to put 'em in the boat."

"Not with me, you don't." I said threateningly.

Larry laughed. "Well, if you don't want to ride with 'em, I guess you could jump out."

He knew very well I wasn't about to touch the water. I tucked my feet under me. "You keep them back there with you then." He couldn't paddle fast enough for me.

*****

It was about 5:30 when Francis pulled into the driveway. He didn't think anything about Catherine being in the yard until she started running toward the car. He swung open the door. "What's wrong?" The worry in her eyes startled him.

"Francis, I can't find Diane anywhere. I haven't seen her since lunch."

"Where have you looked?"

"I checked everywhere. She's not in her bedroom or the shop. She's not in the front or the backyard. There's no sign of her anywhere!" Catherine's frantic voice caused his heart to race.

Francis thought for a moment. "Where's Larry?"

"He went fishing earlier."

He grabbed her arms and lowered his head. "Maybe Diane's with him."

"No. He was taking the canoe. You know she can't swim. She wouldn't have gone with him."

Francis turned toward the bridge down the road. "When did he leave?"

"Right after lunch." He immediately started running toward the bayou. He heard Catherine yelling behind him.

"Wait! I'm coming with you."

He could see the dock just past the bridge and before the bait shop. The pirogue was gone. He grabbed Catherine's hand in his and pulled her into the bait shop.

"Bert, have you seen Larry?"

"Yeah, he took 'dat pirogue out earlier." Bert shook his head. "They've been gone long time, 'dough. Should've been back by now."

"They? Was Diane with him?" Francis asked.

"Yep, just the two of 'em."

Catherine gasped beside him and he saw the horror in her face. Terror gripped his insides.

Francis turned to Bert, "You have another boat we can take to look for them?"

"Sure. It's 'dat udder one at 'da dock. Let me get 'da key."

Hand in hand, Francis and Catherine followed Bert to the dock. Francis could see movement close to the water. He heard Diane scream. Reaching the wooden walkway, they saw Larry helping Diane out of the boat. Larry touched a wire-net full of crawfish to Diane's leg. She screamed again and jumped. Then both she and Larry noticed the three of them approaching.

"Hi, Mom, I've got dinner," Larry announced while tying the pirogue to the dock.

Catherine grabbed Diane by the arm. "You didn't tell me you were going with your brother. I've been searching all over for you!" Then she drew her close.

"I thought you'd know I went with Larry. He said he might take me."

Francis, whose heart had been sinking, felt so relieved that no discipline seemed necessary.

Larry handed Catherine a cloth with something in it. "We brought you some sassafras roots, Mom. You can make us some sassafras tea."

She placed her hand on his shoulder. "Thank God you're both okay."

Bert, who was Cajun through and through, spoke up. In his overalls and straw hat, he turned to Larry, "Next time you take 'da pirogue out, Son, don't stay out dare so long, ya' hear?"

"That looks like quite a catch," Francis said as the four of them walked home.

*****

The school bus stopped in front of the house. Larry and Diane climbed aboard as Catherine waved from the porch. Both her children were adapting well to their new schools in New Orleans. Catherine swept the porch around the Jack-O-Lanterns. Today was Halloween. Larry and his friends were going to take Diane trick-or-treating tonight. She had scraped out a couple of pumpkins to make pies, and the kids carved them into Jack-O-Lanterns.

When she went back inside, Francis was descending the stairs. "You're up early," she said, noticing his uncombed hair. He usually slept later since he worked the second shift at Boeing.

Francis met her at the door and pulled her into his arms. "Hey, Kid." He glanced above her head and out the glass of the door. "They both left for school, huh?" His eyes widened and he raised his eyebrows. "We're all alone." She felt his hands slip down below her waist. "Come back to bed with me," he coaxed, his eyes twinkling mischievously. "We have all morning." He kissed her, but she pulled away slightly.

"I don't have all morning. I have to bake pies, do laundry..." she stopped and laughed, then put her arms around his neck. *Yes, life can wait, can't it?* Her lips met his with urgency. She let him lead her away back up the stairs to their bedroom. The blinds were pulled down, keeping the room dimly lit. She shed her slippers, he removed her robe, and they fell on the bed.

Afterward, she nestled next to him for a little while.

Just before lunch, Catherine fried Francis some bacon and eggs. In a few short hours, he would be leaving for work and the kids would return from school, but first, he was going to call his mother. October 31st was her birthday. It was nice having a telephone in the house again, even if it belonged to Mrs. Landry. Catherine could hear him talking to his mom. He wished her a happy birthday and talked about the Cuban Missile Crisis that ended a few days ago. Then he started talking about the kids and school. Catherine leaned against the kitchen doorframe and watched his face brighten with excitement.

"I told you she was smart. No, I said straight As. The complete report card—all As." There was a pause while Anna Burch responded.

"Well, I bet you never had a kid that did that!" he blurted. Catherine flinched. *He must not have realized what he said.* In a few seconds, he started laughing. "Okay, okay. Yeah, I'm your kid! Well, you didn't, did you?"

Catherine grinned and returned to the kitchen.

*****

Dad took Larry and me to do our Christmas shopping at Katz drug store. I didn't know what to buy Mommy. I walked up and down the aisles looking for that special gift. I asked Larry for ideas, but when he pointed to a thimble, I knew I couldn't listen to him. Finally, I spied a pair of ceramic kittens. They were sitting up on their hind legs and had wiry whiskers that grew from their ceramic flesh. I loved kittens. They were purr-fect! I loved Christmas. Christmas was the greatest time of year.

The next day in school, my teacher handed me a book with an attention-grabbing cover. On it, Santa was standing on a rooftop with eight tiny reindeer. I had never read it before, but I was quickly hooked. Within its clever rhymes resided hope, warmth, and happiness. It made me smile. I knew Christmas was really about Jesus's birthday, but Santa seemed more magical.

On Christmas Eve, we watched *The Beverly Hillbillies* and I reread "'Twas The Night Before Christmas" by Clement Clarke Moore. I couldn't sleep because I knew sometime in the night, my parents were going to put gifts from "Santa" under the tree. I wished very hard for my own bicycle. Surely, my mom and dad were going to give me a bike for Christmas. It was no secret that I wanted one more than anything. I finally fell asleep, and I think sugar plums danced in my head.

When I awoke, there was no bicycle under the tree, but I couldn't wait for Mom to open her kittens.

*****

February 1963

The sun brightened Larry's room as I entered it. I was returning his American History text book. "Puff the Magic Dragon" played on his radio.

"Oh, I love this song," I said, handing him his book.

"I can't believe you read this thing. It's two inches thick!"

"So? I don't care. It's good." I think he believed I was just pretending to like it, but that book actually was on my list of favorites.

"Do you even understand it?" he asked.

"Of course, I do. I read all about the pilgrims, the thirteen colonies, King Edward, the Boston Tea Party, and Paul Revere's famous ride—the British are coming. It's a real page-turner! I'm on chapter eight: George Washington at the Potomac. I'll read more tomorrow." Larry shook his head.

When I left his room, I was on a mission. I needed to ring Mrs. Landry's doorbell and ask her if the new McCall's magazine had arrived. She usually let me have it first so I could cut out the paper doll and clothes to play with them. I had every doll from every magazine she had received. Life was pretty near perfect.

*****

With Diane looking on, Catherine sat at the sewing machine, putting the finishing touches on a skirt. Francis wanted the two of them to go to the French Quarter this Friday night.

"Mom, can't we go to Mardi Gras? Larry gets to go. Why does he get to go?" Catherine heard the pleading in her youngest one's voice.

"I told you before, no. We'll go to the bazaar tomorrow. That'll be fun."

"But I want Mardi Gras beads."

"Larry will bring you some. He's going this weekend." Mardi Gras was exciting with all the parades, colorful costumes, and masquerades. All of New Orleans buzzed with jazz. "You go on outside and play."

Friday evening arrived, and Larry agreed to stay with Diane. Catherine looked at herself in the mirror. The dress she had sewn looked all right. She was excited to be getting out and spending some time with Francis alone. When they first married, most people might not have realized Francis was younger than her. Now that he was thirty-six and she was fifty, it was becoming more noticeable.

When the two of them left that evening, she forgot about their ages. Francis

95

reached for her hand as they drove to the French Quarter in New Orleans. Their eyes met briefly before his had to return to the road. They parked outside a little café on Chartres Street.

"What are you getting?" she asked him after the waiter left them with their menus.

"I'm getting a steak and a potato," he answered while still searching the menu.

"I should've known." This was a special treat. They rarely went out to eat, and this place wasn't cheap.

"Order what you want," he assured her.

After dinner, they strolled onto Bourbon Street. Francis led her into a bar, and they drank a couple of beers. The music wasn't bad, but in a moment, he turned and whispered in her ear. "Let's get out of here."

"Okay." She placed her hand in his and followed him outside.

"I want to go to Jackson Square." He led her down the sidewalk and turned right at the first street.

Catherine pulled her sweater up over her shoulders without putting her arms inside the sleeves. She fastened the top button at the neck. The fullness of her dress swayed just below her knees as she walked. The sun had set, but the evening was comfortable. They walked hand in hand, listening to the music that surrounded them.

Jackson Square in front of the St. Louis Cathedral was an actual block that had flowers and benches, kind of like a park. There were jazz bands on every corner, playing the heart and soul of New Orleans.

One group in particular caught Francis's attention. They had a saxophone, bass, drums, and banjo. In the beginning, he seemed content to stand and watch the musicians play, but when they played "String of Pearls," he couldn't be still any longer. Francis and Catherine danced to several of their tunes. She couldn't remember when she'd had this much fun.

At home, he parked the car and turned off the motor. Moonlight surrounded them. "I really enjoyed tonight," she said.

"Me, too."

*****

May 1963

Diane intently watched her Saturday morning cartoons, and Larry still slept upstairs. Catherine wanted him to rest since he'd been sick with asthma this past week. She dried the last dish and placed it on the cabinet shelf in the kitchen. *Where is Francis? He should've been home hours ago.* Worry predominated. *Has he been in a car accident, or has something else happened?* She couldn't subdue the fear of an affair.

She looked out the window at the yard. Unlike the last couple of months, there

97

were no cars parked there. About two months ago, Francis ran across a '57 Pontiac that wouldn't run. The owners just wanted to get rid of it. He knew it only needed a water pump, so he bought it for next to nothing. He fixed the car and then sold it for a profit. That started a chain reaction of him buying cars, making repairs, and then selling them. When the last person wanted to buy the very car he was driving, he sold it, leaving himself without wheels. He told Catherine he'd rent one until he found them a new car. She learned a long time ago that once he set his mind on something, no one could deter him from his plan.

He should've been home from work around one in the morning, but it was ten o'clock now and there was still no sign of him. She noticed a taxi slowing down outside. It pulled in the driveway, and when she saw Francis get out, she ran to the front door to meet him.

"What happened? Are you all right?" She held the door open. He entered, glancing at her only briefly. He was shaking and pale. She watched as he turned the television off and sent Diane upstairs. Running his hands through his hair, he fell into the chair.

"Francis? Where's the rental car?"

"I wrecked it." He still didn't look at her, but she knew he was worried, though thankfully unharmed.

"What do you mean you wrecked it? How? Where?"

He shook his head. "I don't really remember."

"How could you not remember?"

He looked at her now. "I was drunk. They kept me overnight. The car's impounded, I think."

She took a deep breath and braced herself for the worst. "Where did it happen?"

"I'd just left Bourbon Street."

She knew he loved the music in Jackson Square, but this didn't make sense.

"You don't understand. I don't have insurance for the car."

She remained silent, processing the facts. He didn't come home last night. He went to the French Quarter where he drank too much and wrecked the car, which they didn't own and didn't insure.

"Was anyone hurt?" she managed.

"No, I think I hit a pole or something."

"Did they arrest you?"

He shook his head. "No, just held me overnight."

She kept her distance. She didn't rub his shoulders or kiss his cheek or console him at all. Instead, she softly spoke, "How much damage to the car do you think was done?"

He shook his head. "The money we have set aside for buying a car—it'll probably take all of that. I just don't know."

"Francis, what are we going to do? You have to have a car."

"You don't think I know that? Believe me, I know."

She felt like yelling, "Then why did you get drunk and crash the car?" but she refrained and sighed instead. She had thought life in New Orleans would be good.

*****

Francis opened the envelope from McDonnell Aircraft with anticipation. The letter began like any other, formal and curt. It wasn't until the last paragraph where he read the words "pleased to offer" that he allowed himself to breathe. This was good news and the noted increase in salary, even better.

In recent weeks, prospects for the continuation of his project in New Orleans seemed doomed. He feared he would soon be out of a job. When the government granted the contract for the new Gemini to McDonnell Aircraft in St. Louis, he applied almost immediately. If accepted, they would live just three hours away from his parents.

Since the accident, he hadn't been happy in New Orleans. He'd paid for the rental car and bought an old Cadillac that was in good shape, but he knew Catherine was disappointed in him. Sometimes, he felt like a child and she was his mom. He hated that. Still, they were a family, and he was the breadwinner. Now, they could all move to St. Louis and not only be closer to his family, but hers as well. He knew this would please her.

The only problem was that they had no furniture and no money with which to buy any. Mrs. Landry's house had come completely furnished, which made it perfect for them. He wasn't sure what they would do in St. Louis.

Chapter Eight
Summer 1963

Francis unlocked the front door to the Morrison's house in Crest Wood, a suburb of St. Louis. Catherine followed him inside along with Diane and Larry.

"Wow!" he heard Diane say. "Are the Morrisons rich people?"

Catherine told her, "You be very careful and don't touch things."

Francis looked at the immaculate living room with plush furniture and curio cabinets of precious novelties, before checking out the dining room. The china cabinet was full of expensive dishes. He'd never owned dining room furniture of this caliber.

"Look! They left a six-pack of RC Cola," Larry called out from the kitchen.

Catherine added, "Yes, and they told us to eat anything we wanted, because it won't be good when they return."

Francis looked at Diane. "They even said there's a bicycle in the garage for you to ride."

Diane wasn't interested in the bed-rooms, the RC Cola, or anything else. She headed straight for the garage.

Francis noticed the amazement in Catherine's eyes. True, it wasn't their house; they were only caring for it while the Morrisons were in Europe. But, they could enjoy living like the other half even if only for a little while. This would give him more time to save for furniture. The rent wasn't very much since the owners were more interested in someone who would take care of their belongings. When he saw the ad in the St. Louis Post Dispatch, he knew the Morrisons might entrust their home to them if Mrs. Landry would give a glowing recommendation on their behalf.

When Larry went to check out the garage, Francis asked Catherine, "What do you think? Pretty nice, huh?"

She answered with concern. "Francis, what if we break something? I'm afraid to touch anything."

Quickly, he responded, "I think we should live here as if it's ours. After all, we're not destructive." He started glancing around. He raised his brows and his eyes twinkled. "I'm going to find the thermostat. We have central air conditioning, you know. It should be colder in here!"

*****

When the sun awakened me, I rose immediately from under the soft, fluffy covers. Even though it was the middle of summer, my teeth chattered. It felt like icicles could form any moment at the corner of my eyes. Why did the house have to be so cold? I wasted no time dressing. I brushed my hair in front of the dainty mirrored vanity of the girl to whom this room really belonged.

When I finally stepped foot in the garage, I basked in the balmy heat. I found the girl's bike and opened the garage door. In seconds, I was pedaling down the lane with the warm wind in my face. Riding past all the beautiful homes, life was pretty near perfect—mostly because I had what I'd always wished for: a bike.

*****

With the summer over and the return of the Morrisons, Catherine knew their little taste of luxury had definitely ended when they moved into a one-bedroom apartment on the third floor of an older building in the lower rent district of St. Louis. Francis said it was only temporary. Larry wanted to stay with his oldest sister in Illinois, so they were able to save more money by renting a smaller place. Of course, one bedroom meant Diane had to sleep on the couch. The kitchen was so small it practically didn't exist. But, Francis worked the night shift and was making more money than he ever had. Soon, they would move to one of the suburbs. In the meantime, Diane started the third grade and was doing splendidly.

Catherine tied Diane's bow at the back of her dress. "Sit down and eat your oatmeal."

Diane took a bite. "You forgot the sugar."

She ate while watching *Captain Kangaroo* on television. "Who do you suppose that is boys and girls? Why yes, it's Mr. Green Jeans."

"I like Mr. Green Jeans," Diane said with her mouth full of oatmeal.

"And what time is it? Let's check with Grandfather Clock," Captain Kangaroo said.

Catherine interrupted. "You'd better get going. You're going to be late."

"But, this is my favorite part."

Catherine handed Diane her sack lunch. "Sorry, it's time to go." As Catherine watched her daughter walk down the driveway and across the back yard, she thought, *I've been sending kids to school for twenty-seven years now and I still have a while to go.*

*****

On a cold, gray Friday in November, Diane left for school just like always. Catherine did the dishes and tidied the small apartment before cooking Francis his bacon and eggs.

"You know, if you can have things ready, we can leave when I get off work at midnight next Wednesday," he said while eating. He was talking about Thanksgiving, which was next week. They were going to Mountain Grove.

"Okay. Essie said in her letter for us to be sure and plan a night of cards with her and Jim." Living back in Missouri allowed them to see family, and she looked forward to visiting with her sister.

"I like Pitch. It'll be fun." He kissed her, then looked at his watch. "I'd better get in the shower."

She cleared his dishes and turned on the television, waiting for it to warm up. When the picture finally appeared, it was Walter Cronkite. *What's Walter Cronkite doing on television in the middle of the day?*

"From Dallas, Texas, the flash apparently official, President Kennedy died at 1 p.m. Central Standard Time, 2 p.m. Eastern Standard Time, some thirty-eight minutes ago."

Catherine gasped and dropped the glass she held. She fell into the chair in front of the big Zenith box and turned the knob, increasing the volume. She listened as they explained that shots were fired at the presidential motorcade, hitting the president and the governor of Texas. Vice President Lyndon Baines Johnson would be sworn in aboard Air Force One en route back to Washington.

When Francis turned the water in the shower off, Catherine yelled, "Honey, come here! Hurry!" Over the next several minutes, the two of them sat watching the news report in disbelief. By the time Francis left for work, flags everywhere waved at half-mast as the entire nation mourned. It seemed just yesterday they watched this president put their fears at rest over the Cuban Missile Crisis. He fought for civil rights and championed the space program on which Francis depended. The special news bulletin played films of President Kennedy, Jackie, and their two children playing in the White House. He was certainly too young to have met such a fate. Catherine's heart ached for his family and a country whose path seemed lost without its leader.

At 3:30 that afternoon, Diane opened the apartment door. "Mommy, did you hear?" she asked with her face drawn in distress. "Why would someone shoot President Kennedy?"

Catherine pulled her into her arms and patted her shoulder. "Did they tell you in school?"

"Yeah, we listened to the radio all afternoon. I felt so bad; I just put my head down on my desk."

"Put your books away and I'll make you a snack. We'll watch the news together."

The next three days were sorrowful, and Catherine cried when she watched little

John Jr. salute the casket during the procession.

Wednesday night after work, Catherine, Francis, and Diane left for Mountain Grove. It was after the Thanksgiving meal at the Burches that the telephone rang.

"It's for you," Anna told Catherine. "It's LouAnn."

Startled, Catherine took the receiver. "LouAnn, Honey, is everything okay?"

"Oh, Mother, I thought I might be able to reach you there. Isn't it just awful about President Kennedy?" Catherine and Francis still didn't have a telephone and it was good to hear LouAnn's voice, but it cracked slightly.

"Oh, yes, Honey, it is."

"You know his plane first landed at Meacham Field in Fort Worth?"

"Yes."

"Well, I took Paul and we went to see him." Paul was LouAnn's two-year-old son. "There were several people there to greet the president. Oh, Mom, he shook Paul's little hand before he boarded the plane for Dallas." LouAnn sniffed. "I ran an errand, and by the time I got home and turned on the television, he had died." Catherine could hear LouAnn crying at the other end.

"Oh, Honey, I'm so sorry. I know it's a day you'll never forget."

"I can't sleep, Mom. I just keep seeing him over and over again. To think that was the last hour he lived."

"I know, Baby. It's all so very sad." Catherine talked a few more minutes, consoling her daughter.

"Well, LouAnn, we'd better get off of here. You're going to have a big bill."

"Okay, Mom. I'll write soon."

*****

December 1963

Snow covered the ground as the Christmas holidays approached. On Christmas Eve, I read "Twas the Night before Christmas" more than once. In fact, I memorized it. I was thankful our little apartment only had one bedroom, requiring me to nestle down on the couch close to the Christmas tree. I pretended to be asleep so I could see what my parents gave me from Santa. I wished for a bike again this year.

When I awoke sometime later, the room was dark. I could faintly see the shimmer of the tinsel on the tree. I strained to see if anything new had been added underneath, but it was too dark. I believed I could see a shiny fender. Yes, it could be the shape of a bicycle beside the tree. My parents were light sleepers, so there was no checking it out before morning. When the time finally arrived and light filled the room, there was no sign of a bicycle.

*****

Catherine knew how much Diane wanted a bike. Francis always said they didn't have the money, but he spent money on the things he wanted.

That January, Francis chose a house in St. Charles on a golf course. It had three bedrooms, two bathrooms, and a basement. It had a huge back yard, but Catherine was mostly thankful for the washer and dryer. She knew Francis liked this location because it wasn't too far from Lambert Field and McDonnell Aircraft. He didn't play golf, so that wasn't it.

They picked up some necessary pieces of secondhand furniture. Francis said they were saving up to purchase better furnishings, but one night after work, he carried in a new electric Gibson guitar and amplifier.

"Check this out," he told her. "Look at the neck on this guitar."

"Yeah, what does that mean?"

"See how small it is? It'll be perfect for learning, easy to wrap your fingers around on the frets."

Catherine didn't know how much it cost and she didn't ask because she didn't want to dampen his excitement.

"I can teach Diane to play," he continued.

"Does she want to play?"

"Of course, she does. You saw that letter the school sent home saying she had musical talent." He stared at her in disbelief.

"Oh...well...I think that'll be great."

Over the next several months, Francis started teaching Diane chords on the guitar, and she seemed to pick it up quickly. Soon, he added another guitar, a fiddle, and a mandolin to his music arsenal along with a fancy recording device. He and Diane played for hours and he recorded it. He would show her new notes and changes. They played songs like the "St. Louis Blues," "Whispering," and "Your Cheating Heart." The instruments were expensive, but seeing Francis and Diane spending time together made Catherine happy. Already in the fourth grade, Diane was growing up quickly.

One morning, Catherine poured Francis's coffee and sat across the table from him.

"You know, September's coming up. I was thinking maybe we could get Diane a bicycle for her birthday or even Christmas," she ventured.

"I don't think we can afford it." He continued eating.

"But she was so disappointed last Christmas."

"Bicycles are pricey. Maybe for her next birthday."

Catherine wished she could get Diane a bike somehow, but there were many things their daughter didn't have.

"She also wants a Barbie Doll. All the other kids have one."

"I don't know. We'll see."

Catherine had always found ways to see that her children had certain things. She sewed them new clothes for the start of a school year. When she lived on the farm, she managed to save egg money or some kind of change. Then she would surprise her sons or daughters, by providing whatever they needed. Francis didn't give her money and there were no opportunities to save some change, except when she did laundry. Very seldom did he leave any change in his pockets. He paid the bills. He even went with her to the grocery store. His money was just that—his.

Then, a thought occurred to her. Each time they bought groceries and even gas, the merchants gave S&H Green Stamps. She always pasted them into the books and saved them, accumulating enough to redeem for merchandise. She decided to look in the S&H Green Stamp catalog for Barbie Dolls.

One Saturday, when Francis had an errand to run, Catherine decided not to wait for Christmas. She and Diane went with him downtown. While he shopped, they went to the redemption center. Catherine let her daughter pick out the Barbie Doll and case she wanted. Most girls bought dresses and accessories for their dolls, but they only had enough stamps for the doll and case. Diane's Barbie came with only a red swim suit and slip on heels to match. Catherine would have to sew its clothes. It pleased her to see Diane's excitement.

Once home, Catherine took some pieces of black felt and some fur from some old slippers. She cut and sewed them into a coat with a fur collar for Barbie. Then she took various colors of silk scraps, lace, and netting and sewed ball gowns. She presented them to Diane with a smile.

"Oh, Mommy, they're beautiful!" Diane hugged her, which was sufficient payment for the painstaking detail required for such small garments. Diane played for hours, sometimes starting as early as six o'clock in the morning.

Catherine understood Francis's love for music and his desire to own musical things, but when he purchased a fishing boat, though they still needed better furniture, she started to see a selfishness she had ignored before.

However, at a reunion with her children, those musical instruments and that fishing boat brought the family closer together. Wallace, Audrey, Linda, and Buck all came with their families. Larry had joined the Navy and was home from boot camp. Even though LouAnn wasn't able to come, it was wonderful having the rest of them all together again. Buck and Larry played harmonicas, and Francis played guitar, fiddle, and mandolin. With his reel-to-reel tape deck, Francis recorded each member of the family singing or performing in some way.

They all went fishing on the Gasconade River. During the summer reunion at Table Rock Lake, they used the boat to fish and waterski. Any time they gathered, music always played a part and Catherine reveled in the nearness of her children.

Eventually, Francis did buy new furniture for every room in the house, and he gave Diane a new bicycle for her eleventh birthday.

Chapter Nine
1965

Shortly after Diane's birthday, Francis got a wild hair to try his hand at farming. Catherine tried to be supportive. They moved into a huge two-story farmhouse on twenty-seven acres in Jonesburg, which was about seventy miles west of St. Louis. They planted a fairly large garden and bought a few head of cattle. He purchased hay and put it away in the barn for winter. But since he went to work every afternoon and slept late in the mornings, it was Catherine who did the farming. Reminiscent of a previous life, her back ached, and many times, that pain forced her to lay flat on the floor for relief.

Every afternoon, Francis left for work in their brand new Mercury. When the snows came, she found herself putting out hay and salt, and rounding up the steers with the help of Diane's dog, Oscar. They adopted him after he'd suddenly appeared at Essie and Jim's farm. Oscar, a Collie-English Shepherd mix, was well trained, so they were happy to bring him home after a visit to Essie's. Besides, Diane had always wanted a dog.

Unfortunately, that winter was one of the coldest Catherine had seen since moving back to Missouri and that made tending the farm more difficult for her.

*****

I remember the first time I entered our big house on the farm. The tour included the attic, which was a room on the second level that contained a wheelchair. The man to whom it belonged died of tuberculosis right there in the house. I shuddered looking at it. My bedroom was on the first floor behind the entryway and the staircase that led upstairs.

One night when I went to bed, I heard a sound on the staircase. Then I heard it again, like someone slowly going up the stairs, one foot after the other. I thought it must be my imagination.

Every night I heard it, and every night I told myself it was my imagination. But fear always seized me, clutching its gnarly claws around my lungs so that I couldn't breathe. If not my imagination, then what was it? Maybe it was the spirit of the old man who had died. My body shook and my teeth chattered. Many nights, I feigned illness so Mom would come and stay with me awhile. Yet, every morning the sun would rise and all would be okay. It was just my imagination after all, but it seemed so real.

That Christmas, we went out in our woods and cut down our own tree. Dad gave me a Timex watch. When spring finally arrived, he bought me a softball and glove and taught me how to catch. Then he taught me how to bat. We had always been St. Louis Cardinals fans. Whenever the game wasn't televised, he and I would listen to it on the radio. I always liked it when Bob Gibson pitched, but my favorite player was Orlando Cepada, the first baseman.

*****

March 1966

On Sunday, Francis drove into Jonesburg to a local café. He often went there on weekends to get a cup of coffee and visit with other farmers. The waitress, whose daughter went to school with Diane, usually flirted with him. He flirted back. It didn't mean anything, but he enjoyed it.

After a bit, he left for home. The railroad tracks ran along the road and he heard a train whistle. He thought to himself, *That darn train will probably be crossing the road when I turn and I'll have to wait.* But today, he flinched when he heard a loud screeching sound and a horrible thud followed by the awful sound of twisting metal. He pushed down on the accelerator. By the time he turned, the train had almost stopped, and debris lined the track, evidence of what used to be a car.

He jumped out and started running along the track, thinking someone might need help. He saw torn clothing stained with blood. The body of a young boy lay on the ground, but he was gone. Pain stabbed Francis's chest and he gagged as he saw mangled hair and arms. The sight was horrendous. He felt the blood drain from his face and sink to his shoes. He struggled to stand. Others arrived at the scene, people more experienced in emergencies. His knees buckled beneath him and he fell to the ground. Sitting there, numb, he listened to those around him. Someone mentioned the last name of the victims, saying there were four souls in all. He wanted to cry, but tears wouldn't come.

Later, when he returned home, he saw Catherine cooking in the kitchen. Her eyes met his.

"What's wrong?" she asked. "You look like you've seen a ghost."

He didn't answer because the words wouldn't come. His body moved about as if it were an empty shell. His eyes beheld, yet didn't see. His ears heard, yet he couldn't comprehend.

"Are you alright? Francis?"

*****

Today, Amy returned to school for the first time since it happened. Her mother, two sisters, and brother were killed in a train wreck. It was the saddest thing I ever heard.

Only a few weeks before, it was her mother who gave me the cupcake with the most icing at our Valentine's party. She even spent time talking to me when few others did. Amy's little sister was beautiful and had long, blonde hair. All the kids in our class adored her.

The day of the accident, Amy, who was ill, stayed home from church with her father. Her mom, sixteen-year-old big sister, twelve-year-old big brother, and five-year-old little sister, were all in the car. Dad, being the first one on the scene, said he'd never seen such a horrific sight. My heart went out to my friend and her father. The train's engineer said the car stopped, but then started again and stalled on the tracks. Mom said Dad was never the same after that.

I thought a lot about death. That Sunday morning, Amy's family didn't know their lives would soon be over. I realized you didn't have to be old to die. You could be sixteen or twelve or even five. It occurred to me that death is out of our control.

I had spent weeks every summer at my grandparents' house these past few years. We always went to church. Pleasant Hill Baptist Church met in a one-room, rock schoolhouse in the country. I listened as Brother Hudson preached about Jesus not wanting anyone to die in their sin. "Sin separates you from God," he said. In the Old

Testament times, people had to sacrifice choice rams or lambs once every year to receive forgiveness for their sins, but Jesus became the perfect lamb—a one-time sacrifice for all who accept Him.

One night on the farm, while alone in my bed by the window, I looked outside. The stars shined more brightly than usual. The whole sky glowed. It was a glorious night. I remembered a story Aunt Sarie used to read, and a picture of Jesus standing at a door. Could he be standing at the door of my heart and knocking right now? I instantly knew I was a sinner and desperately wanted God's forgiveness. In that moment, I prayed and asked God to forgive me and He did. I didn't worry about what words I said or how I said them. I prayed and He forgave. The next morning, I felt jubilant and light as a feather. I skipped everywhere and even felt like I could fly.

"What's gotten into you?" Mom asked.

I stopped floating long enough to explain. "I don't know, but I think it's because I prayed to God last night and asked Him to forgive me." She started to say something, but I bounced out the door and into the sunshine with my newfound freedom.

That prayer was the single most important decision of my life. I'm so thankful for the year spent on the farm that brought me to God, but I will never forget my friend and her tragedy.

Mom wanted me to talk with my grandparents about my prayer. When we went for a visit, Grandma rejoiced with me, explaining how I had become a Child of the King. She shared with me that she and Grandpa prayed every day that my dad would find Jesus like I had. I had never thought about such things before now. From that time on, I prayed for Dad the same as my grandparents.

"For God so loved the world that he gave his only begotten Son, that whosoever believeth in him should not perish, but have everlasting life. For God sent not his Son into the world to condemn the world, but that the world through him might be saved."

John 3:15-16

*****

After Dad butchered the calves, we moved from the country back to the city—O'Fallon, Missouri. One day while I was at school, my parents returned to the farm to visit its new residents.

When I came home, Mother told me that the woman had removed the carpet from the stairs. One afternoon, she noticed footprints in the dust on the wooden steps—footprints that led to the attic and back down again. That night, her husband chased someone out of the house with a shotgun. When the sheriff investigated, he found a homeless man who had a key. The man had been entering the house late at night to sleep in the attic. *Wow! I guess it wasn't just my imagination! All those nights it must have been him I was hearing. It wasn't a ghost after all!*

Chapter Ten
1966

  I started sixth grade in O'Fallon. I made friends easily and discovered boys. Bruce sat across from me at lunch and always gave me his chocolate milk because he knew I liked it. He excelled in arithmetic, the same as me. Dad's coworker also lived in O'Fallon. He and his wife had a sixteen-year-old son who had red hair, freckles, and wore glasses. Whenever his parents invited us over, he and I hung out. He taught me to roller skate in their basement. He and I were more than fond of each other. We would sit in his parents' station wagon and plan trips to far off places.

  I liked living on St. Joseph Drive. It was the epitome of community: nicely mowed lawns, backyard barbeques, and friendly people—the life for which I had always longed. Mom met our next-door neighbors, the Greenwalts. She said they were nice and had two sons, but I hadn't seen either of them. Mrs. Greenwalt told Mom the boys were usually busy doing homework.

  One day, I was attempting a hand-stand on the back patio when I heard their backdoor open and close. Two brothers, laughing and dribbling a basket-ball, didn't even notice that I was there. I watched them push and shove and turn and shoot the ball into the hoop above the back of their garage. One was probably three or four years older than me, had dark hair, and wore dark-rimmed glasses. It was the other one who caught my attention. He was about my age, maybe a year older, with blonde hair. I sat down quietly and continued to observe.

The ball would go into the basket and they would start all over again, fighting for possession on their homemade court. The younger one managed to steal the ball, dribble, and turn to shoot. The ball went in the hoop, but he never saw it because he finally noticed me. He stood frozen, staring. I could feel my face growing hot. And then, he smiled. His brother punched him hard on the shoulder, but he had the most beautiful smile I'd ever seen. I couldn't help but giggle.

"John, what's the matter?" his brother scolded him. "You act like you've never seen a girl before."

They resumed their play, but I got the sense John was trying to impress me since he kept glancing in my direction. I played along and became the fan in the stands, applauding him whenever he made a basket or took the ball away.

When his mother called the two of them in for dinner, he came to the chain link fence separating our yards. "Hi, I'm John. You must be the new girl."

I laughed. "I'm Diane, but I don't know about the new part. I've lived here a couple of months now." I became aware of everything: the wayward lock of his hair, my pulse, the cleanliness of my teeth, and the frizziness of my hair.

He laughed nervously. "Really? I've never seen you before." He looked down at the ground before confessing, "I'm usually bogged down with homework."

I decided to change the subject. "Looks like fun out there. I play softball, but I've never actually dribbled a basketball before."

"Oh, yeah? Maybe I can teach you sometime." His mother called him again.

"I'd like that," I yelled as he ran off.

That Saturday, my friend Anne came over to play. Shortly thereafter, Bruce showed up on my front porch unannounced with Craig. I hadn't made the connection that this might have been planned since Craig liked Anne, and Bruce liked me. All I could think about was Dad, who was pacing in the kitchen where he could keep a constant eye on the four of us. Later, I could hear my parents from my bedroom.

"Francis, she's only in the sixth grade. It's all very harmless," Mom pleaded.

"Harmless! Did you see those two boys out there? What's she doing having boys over to the house without asking?" Dad sounded furious, like a dragon breathing fire.

"She didn't know they were coming. What did you expect her to do? She didn't do anything wrong."

Okay, so I learned something—never have a boy over whenever Dad was home!

I thought John had forgotten about teaching me how to dribble, but one Friday night, I answered the door to find him holding a basketball.

"Are you busy?" he asked. "Want to play horse?"

"Excuse me?"

"It's a basketball game. I'll teach you."

"Sure." I was out the door in a flash. We walked through his garage into the back yard. I assumed his parents were home. He threw the ball into the hoop, banking it off the backboard.

"Your turn," he said, handing me the ball. "You have to make the exact same shot from the exact same spot."

"Oh, yeah, sure!" I took the ball, stood where he had stood, and feebly made an attempt to throw it into the basket.

"Here, hold the ball like this," he said, putting his arms around me. He moved my fingers slightly and placed his hands on mine. A strange warmth spread through my hands and into my arms. Then, his hands went up with mine, the ball lifting off and almost landing where it should.

"There, that was better," he encouraged me.

"Thanks. I'll try now. I think I've got it," I assured him. I threw a couple of balls before I got the hang of it. The first game I lost, but afterward, I was definitely a contender. We pushed, shoved, and did a lot of laughing. He made me feel...good.

His parents returned from the grocery store to find us outside. "John, you have chores to do," his mom ordered.

*****

The house in O'Fallon had three bedrooms and two bathrooms. Catherine knew Diane liked riding her bike to school, which was only down the street. Her youngest, now twelve years old, made friends quickly and excelled in school.

"You know, there's a bunch of guys at work who play music," Francis told her while eating his breakfast. "I'm thinking we should have a party."

"That sounds like fun." She dried the skillet and put it away. "Where would we have it?"

He took a sip of coffee. "Well, why couldn't we have it here?"

"Francis, our living room isn't big enough," she protested, but she knew once he set his mind on something, there would be no changing it. Their living room wasn't small, but certainly didn't allow enough space to set up instruments and sound.

"I wasn't thinking of the living room. I'm thinking we'll have it outside under the carport and back patio."

The concrete of the carport ran the full depth of the house and extended farther back and down the side, making a sizable covered patio. "Well, I suppose you could, but what about the neighbors?"

"They'll love it—free music." He raised his eyebrows. "Maybe they'll come join us. There'll be room for dancing. It's a great idea."

It could be fun, she thought, *but if they play too loud or things get crazy, it could mean trouble with the neighbors.*

The next morning, Francis told her he had already invited people to the party, which he was planning for Saturday. She felt her heart race anxiously, but she could see his enthusiasm. They made a list of things they'd need. They only had two days to prepare. She could do this for him. He had invited men who played the bass guitar, the mandolin, the accordion, and the fiddle. They were going to have themselves an old fashioned hoedown!

Everybody started arriving about seven o'clock Saturday evening. There were about twenty guests in all. Francis had lined the carport and patio with special lights, and they'd cleared an area for dancing. Soon, the music started and so did the fun. There were coolers with ice, beer, and soft drinks. Catherine had spent all day making finger foods.

She watched him play. He so enjoyed times like these. He played lead guitar, sometimes rhythm, and other times, the fiddle. Together, all the musicians sounded great—great, but loud. Soon, the accordion took the lead and out rang the polkas. Everyone danced. The party was a great success. As the night progressed and the beers left the coolers, both the crowd and the music got louder and louder.

At about one o'clock in the morning, Catherine was no longer enjoying herself. She worried about the neighbors who might be trying to sleep. She tried to reason with her intoxicated husband, but he became belligerent.

"Francis, the neighbors," she pleaded quietly, trying not to let their guests know.

"You just can't stand it that I'm having fun," he told her. "Don't tell me what to do." His raised voice dashed all hopes of keeping their exchange private. "You just don't like it that I have friends," he slurred the words. "Just because you don't have any friends…"

She turned and saw the horror on Diane's face, but before she could react, she noticed a police car park at the driveway and an officer got out. She quickly excused herself, thinking it would be better if she talked to the policeman herself. She hurried to intercept him before he made it to the back.

"Can I help you, Officer?" she asked.

"Do you live here, Ma'am?"

"Yes, Sir, I do."

"We've had a complaint from some of your neighbors about the noise. You need to end your party now, Ma'am."

"Yes, Sir. We were actually just wrapping up. I'm so sorry." When she returned to the group, she started explaining what the officer said. Most everyone started leaving accordingly, but Francis was convinced she was running off his friends. After their guests left, he spewed obscenities at her and then left on foot.

As she tucked Diane into bed, she explained, "Your father just drank too much. He didn't mean anything he said. He probably won't even remember." Deep inside, though, she wasn't so sure. "You go to sleep. I'm going to get in the car and go find your dad."

Catherine drove up and down the streets of their neighborhood. *How far could he have gotten?* She thought about the events of the evening. It could be the alcohol talking, but she remembered the burning look in his eyes, as if he hated her. She turned right and her headlights illuminated him walking on the side of the road.

She pushed the button and rolled down the passenger window. "Francis, get in." He refused at first, but she finally convinced him. When they got home, it took some coaxing for her to get him to the bedroom and let her remove his shoes. He fell backward and passed out.

The next morning, Catherine felt uneasy. *Why did Francis say all those things? Will he remember what happened? Is our relationship in trouble?* She already had one failed marriage—she needed to keep this one together. Francis should apologize, but she knew he wouldn't.

*****

Francis couldn't believe Catherine asked their guests to leave. It made him mad. He was the one who went to work every day. If he wanted to have a party, what did it matter to her? She was probably the one who called the cops in the first place. She always had to be the voice of reason, ruining any fun he might have.

After work that Tuesday night, he decided to stop at a tavern for a beer. He shot a game of pool with one of the other patrons. In no time, he found himself telling jokes and laughing with two of the women at the bar. One in particular caught his attention. She had thick red hair and an infectious laugh. Before the night ended, they drank a couple of beers and talked about Indie car racing.

"Have you ever been to the Indie 500?" she asked. Her long eyelashes curled up at the end, accentuating her baby blue eyes.

"No, but I wouldn't mind going sometime."

"I'm taking my daughter this year," she told him. "You should go."

"What…? You mean with you?" He was half kidding.

"Why not?" she asked. "It could be fun."

She was flirting with him, and he liked it. If he had to guess, she probably wasn't much younger than him. She'd already told him she was divorced and had a daughter who was fifteen.

He didn't wear a ring on his finger. When he and Catherine married, they didn't have rings or any money with which to buy them. Catherine had continued to wear her old one. Not having a ring didn't bother him.

"I suppose I could drive," he offered. "When were you leaving?" He heard his voice and realized what he had just said. Still, why couldn't he have a little fun? What harm could there be in it? A stolen weekend away with someone who laughed at his jokes—he needed that. It didn't have to go any further, did it?

"I was going to leave next Friday. You free?" Her moist lips curved and he couldn't stop staring at them, wondering how they might taste.

He didn't answer at first. He drained the last of his beer and set the glass on the table. "I can be."

That weekend turned out to be the first of many stolen moments away from the normal grind of family.

*****

Catherine grew more and more concerned. It was Saturday afternoon and Francis hadn't come home from work Friday night. They normally did their grocery shopping on the weekend and the pantry was empty. Francis had their only car. Last night, she'd made Diane the last egg. They had each eaten a Miracle Whip sandwich for breakfast, but by Saturday evening, she and Diane were starving. She had to think of something.

"Do you want to ride your bike and see if you can find any soda bottles?" she asked her daughter.

"Sure."

*****

Mom gave me a cloth bag to hold any bottles I found. The sun was shining, and there was a cool breeze as I rode my bike, searching for empty glass soda bottles people had thrown out the windows of their cars into the grass. My stomach growled as I stopped to get the first one I saw. There was a deposit of three cents per bottle. If I could find enough of them, I could take them to the store, turn them in, and get that deposit back. Mom told me to buy a can of potted meat. It came in a small round can and cost fifteen cents. If I could find five bottles, we could have a potted meat sandwich because there were a few slices of bread left. As I rode, I wondered what Dad was doing. *Why didn't he come home?* Mom was pleased when I finally returned home with a small paper bag. I liked potted meat sandwiches, especially whenever I was hungry.

Dad finally came home on Sunday. He never told me where he'd been. I expected Mom to ask, but she didn't say much at all.

Chapter Eleven

Catherine noticed the sun sink lower in the western sky as a light summer wind blew through the curtains of the windows. Diane and John were in the living room, watching *The Moon Spinners*, a Hayley Mills movie. It was hard for Catherine to realize her daughter was turning thirteen and starting junior high in the fall. Diane was chosen to enter an accelerated program of schooling. John was in the same program, but a year older. It allowed all the students completing their courses through high school to graduate a year early.

Catherine stitched the last of her quilt blocks together, finishing the sixth quilt top. Of course, she'd have to talk Francis into buying the fill and backing she needed to complete all of them. Lately, it seemed like he didn't have any money for anything.

She knew about his drinking and poker playing. Sometimes, he'd lose track of time or end up sleeping it off in his car. This usually happened on the weekends and had become quite a habit. She wondered if he could be seeing someone else. That thought gnawed at her. What would she do if he left her? Francis was all she had. But, he was crazy about Diane and vice-versa. Maybe that would be enough for him.

Since Francis worked the second shift, on the weekdays, he wouldn't usually get home until midnight or one o'clock in the morning. This summer, Diane had been staying up late, watching the late movie. Catherine suspected her of staying awake so she and her dad could talk when he got home because he wasn't around on the weekends. Sometimes, in the afternoons, they'd play music together, Diane on rhythm guitar and him on lead guitar or fiddle.

On Saturday, Francis left in the morning to get the car serviced, but he'd been gone for hours now. She sighed. He probably wouldn't return home before tomorrow evening.

She needed to cook something for dinner. She'd better see if anything was in the icebox. As she walked to the kitchen, she observed Diane and John and heard them talking in an English accent. Catherine shook her head. Funny how when the Greenwalts found out Diane was accepted into the accelerated program, they'd let John have more freedom around her.

*****

1967

I didn't really mind that Dad worked nights because whenever he was home, he decided what we'd watch on TV. Dad would never have let me watch the two new shows,

Room 222 and *The Monkees*, and he would not have let me watch *The Moon Spinners*, especially with John. But Dad wasn't home, and John and I liked *The Moon Spinners*.

It turned out that John not only played basketball, but he didn't have a problem pretending either. In fact, his imagination matched my own. In my mind, I could be whatever I wanted, facing whatever conflicts and solving them heroically. John was right there with me.

When the movie ended, we decided to be Hayley Mills (Nikki) and Peter McEnery (Mark) overcoming the bad guys and returning the stolen jewels. It was the patio scene after Nikki had just met Mark and learned the legend of the Moon Spinners.

"Oh, Mauc, luk at the mune," I said, looking dreamily into the ceiling as if the moon were there. "That's what I want to be."

"What's that?" John asked, in a perfect English accent.

"A moon spinner, spinning and spinning, making a purr-fect moon."

John moved closer, just like Mark did in the movie. "What a romantic you are, Nikki." I dropped character, staring at his lips. I couldn't remember what to say. His eyes were staring into mine. His lips parted and he drew a slow breath. "Good night," he finished. I nodded, entranced. He was going to kiss me. I closed my eyes.

"Diane, I'm cooking hamburgers for dinner," Mom said from the entrance to the living room, bringing us back to reality.

*****

Catherine went to bed, but she couldn't sleep. *Is Francis really out drinking and gambling or has someone else captured his attention?* Almost every weekend, he either didn't come home at all or wandered off for part of it. His love had always made her feel secure until recently. Deep down, she knew what his behavior indicated. *Is it happening all over again?*

She knew it was time to confront him, but she couldn't have dreaded anything more. *What if he doesn't love me*? She couldn't bear that. She still loved him. *What can I do? Where will I go*? She was fifty-three years old. Buying a box of Clairol's color had become a necessity about every three months. Still, she didn't believe her age was the problem. He still desired her at times. That fact gave her a glimmer of hope and the courage to talk to him.

Sunday evening, he returned, not offering any explanation for his absence. She watched him closely. He changed the channel on the television. Then he picked up his guitar, plugged it into the amplifier, and started strumming melodies.

When Diane left to go play with some friends, Catherine sat in the chair across from him. Her hands trembled and her heart raced. She felt nauseated. He continued to ignore her. He stroked the strings and fingered a familiar tune.

Catherine took in a deep breath and then exhaled. "What's her name?"

He stopped playing and looked at her, his blue eyes piercing her heart. "Who?"

"The one who's taking you away from me—the one who's taking you away from your daughter." It took all her strength, but her eyes never left his.

"What?" He looked surprised. "No one's taking me away." She noticed his hands started shaking. He turned his head and wouldn't look at her.

"Something is. I want to know what you're doing." She made the statement, but she wasn't sure she wanted to know at all.

He stood and started pacing. She wished she hadn't charted this course. She wasn't prepared to lose her husband. If only he'd grab her, hold her close, and tell her it was all a mistake.

"I'm not any different than I've ever been."

"Francis, you're practically not home at all on the weekends. Diane stays awake at night to see you when you get off work because you're not here except during the week. What happens when the school year starts? Will she never see you?"

He flinched. She had struck a nerve. He sat and stared at the floor. There was an awkward silence. Catherine froze, not willing to pry further.

The front door unlatched and Diane dashed in all out of breath. "You should have seen me, Dad! I hit a home run and we had the bases loaded!"

Francis's eyes never left Catherine's as he responded to his daughter. "That's good," he said. "You want to play some music?"

"Yeah, let me get a drink first."

*****

Francis steered the car onto Interstate 70. Even though it was Friday, there wouldn't be much traffic at 2 a.m. Had he done the right thing? She had cried when he told her. No, of course, he did what he had to do. He felt lighter, like losing a heavy weight he'd been carrying. Still, an incredible sadness enveloped him. That chapter of his life was over and done. In the beginning, it had been like an adventure, exciting and alluring, but recently, their rendezvous became seductive and exotic. Like an addiction, he'd found himself looking forward to their next blissful encounter.

Sometimes, life suffocated him. He'd stolen weekends away to feel young and free again. At least, that's the way it started. She'd almost persuaded him to forever alter the path of his life in pursuit of fun with this beautiful redhead. When he was with Catherine, life was about obligations, but even so, he wasn't willing to walk away from his life with his wife and little girl.

Some of the guys at work had been talking about job opportunities at Northrup in California. Maybe that was what he needed—sunny California. The springs and summers in Missouri were all right, but if he never saw snow and ice in the winter again, that would suit him just fine. Catherine would like it there. Maybe they could start over. Francis hadn't told her yet, but he had talked to Northrup's personnel department and sent them the information they had requested. There was no sense in saying anything until he knew if he had a job or not.

He pulled into the driveway of their O'Fallon home and his spirits lifted. He noticed a light from the lamp in the living room and smiled. The school year started last week, but on this Friday night, Diane had probably stayed awake until he got home.

*****

Catherine awoke early that Saturday while Francis and Diane still slept. In the quiet of the kitchen, she sipped her coffee. A fog lingered in the back yard. She thought about her life—fifty-four years of events—events that had led her here. She knew her marriage was in danger, and she knew she must do something.

She missed her Ozark hills of Wright County and her dearest sister, Essie. Oh, to be able to talk to Essie, to ask her for advice. No, she could never talk to anyone about the problems in her marriage, certainly not her children or her closest sister. They had been there when her first marriage ended, her children suffering the fallout. She knew God had never left her, but couldn't bring herself to ask him for help. After all, this was her mess, the results of her decisions.

Catherine remembered the night she met Francis. They had eyes only for each other. He had soothed her broken heart as they danced in each other's arms. She remembered their picnic under the glow of the autumn sun beside a gentle stream. He captured her with his charm. She thought about that day when he showed up on her doorstep. She had been trying to resist seeing him, but that had prompted a sorrow deeper than despair. More than anything else, she had wanted to see him, feel his arms around her, let his guitar music take her away. As the radio played "Sunny Side of the Street," she had opened the door to find him beckoning her to "come out and play" and that was exactly what she needed.

She took another sip of her coffee. Those days were long gone. She heard a noise and turned to see Francis staring at her.

"I couldn't sleep. The coffee smells too good to pass up," he said.

The words were casual, but seriousness dwelt in his eyes.

"I'll pour you a cup."

"Sit down," he said, taking the cup from her. "We need to talk."

She shook on the inside as she sat across from him. In that moment, she felt every bit of her fifty-four years. She could feel the crinkling of the wrinkles around her eyes and the slight bulging of her waistline as she looked at her forty-one-year-old husband. Never had she been this tired.

"I applied for a job in California."

These were not the words she expected. "What? I mean, you did what?"

"There's a company called Northrup in L.A. who's hiring. They want me to be there next month."

As Catherine slowly processed this information, questions screamed in her head. *Is he leaving us? If not, how are we getting there? Is Diane supposed to leave her school and friends again?* "What about Diane and me?"

"You'll both love it there." He was smiling now. "The sun shines all the time, even at Christmas!"

"Francis, Diane's in an advanced program at school. We shouldn't take her out of it." Obviously, he hadn't thought about this. "She loves it *here*."

"I'm sure California schools will have a similar program to this one."

She thought for a moment, then, "I would love to see California, but not when Diane has so much going for her here. She's in junior high, you know." The color in his face drained, showing his disappointment in her lack of enthusiasm about yet another move that would take them a world away.

Silence lingered for too long. Catherine realized Francis had considered only himself in this decision. He had figured she and Diane would adjust like they'd always done.

His eyes moved from his coffee cup to stare straight into hers. "Remember when you asked who was taking me away from you?"

Her heart beat a warning so loudly she could hardly breathe. "Yes," she whispered.

"Well, there was someone."

There it was—her biggest fear. She loved him, supported him in bad as well as good times, and this was her reward. She looked at his wavy locks of hair, his blue eyes, and his handsome face. She wanted to scream or at least run out of the room.

Instead, she ventured, "Who is she? Do I know her?" Her voice was barely audible.

"No." He placed his hand on hers. "She didn't mean anything. We just had some laughs."

"You had some laughs! You had some laughs?" There was her voice, but she couldn't prevent her hands from trembling and pulled her hand away from his.

"Yes, we had some laughs." He held his head high, defiantly. "You know, we don't laugh anymore—you and me." Then he stood and looked down at her.

"Yeah, well whose fault is that? Mine?" She stood, also, but he was still eight inches taller.

He paused before he continued in a softer tone. "I think California will be good for us. It would be better if we got away from here. And they're sending movers that will pack us and move everything."

She didn't want to fight anymore, and she didn't want to acknowledge his affair. At least he confessed. Kenneth never did. No, she still loved Francis even after this revelation.

She surrendered to his arms as he pulled her in, but his embrace wasn't as sweet as before. She remembered that night long ago when she found out the difference in their ages. She had tried to reason with him, saying he could have any number of other girls. He had replied that she was the only one he wanted. How she ached to hear that now.

Chapter Twelve

The movers stacked the boxes high and created a maze in the living room through which Catherine maneuvered. When she reached the front door, the massive moving van in the street confirmed again that yes, indeed, she was moving. Soon, they would load the living room suite Francis bought two years ago, along with the two bedrooms of new furniture, Diane's bicycle, and all their worldly possessions into that North American Van Lines truck, and the drivers would head for the west coast. Then she, Diane, and Francis would drive their red Mercury. They would go through Mountain Grove and visit the Burches before starting their 1500-mile trek on Route 66. She couldn't help but be a little excited.

It was a warm day in October and the leaves on the trees had started changing. She noticed Diane and John talking and laughing under one of them. She looked up and down the street at their neighbors' homes, and felt a pang of regret. She had thought for sure that they would be happy here. At one point, she believed they were. Well, Diane was happy. She had proved to be a bright student at Fort Zumwalt Junior High and, unfortunately, had become rather close to John.

Catherine hadn't always prayed like she should have in these last years, but fearing Diane had the most to lose in moving to California, she turned to God. She didn't pray for her relationship with Francis because she felt unworthy to pray about that. She prayed about Diane.

Two weeks ago, Diane came home excited about an assignment for English class. She had to write an essay about an imaginary trip to a place she wanted to go, using a map to plot the directions. Diane didn't know at the time they were moving, but she wrote her paper about a trip to Los Angeles, traveling on Route 66. Catherine thought maybe that was a sign from God.

Her relationship with Francis was precarious at best. Maybe he was right and a move was what they needed. Maybe they'd find happiness in the golden state. Francis always spoke fondly of it. He appeared to be trying. Lately, he'd been playing a new song on the guitar entitled "Almost Persuaded." Its lyrics spoke about a man who was almost persuaded to kiss the lips of another, but instead returned to his loving wife. Catherine hoped Francis's behavior had not been more than a man in his forties temporarily losing his way.

*****

At first, I didn't really believe we were moving to L.A., home of Beverly Hills, swimming pools, and movie stars! I had visions of becoming a movie star. I loved acting. I didn't really think about changing schools. What bothered me most were the friends I'd be leaving. Anne told me goodbye this morning. She even gave me her ruby bracelet that I'd always admired. We both cried. I knew I'd really miss her. Now, John and I were spending all the time we had left with each other.

I leaned against the tree trunk. Autumn leaves fell around us in a gentle breeze. "Who's going to help me with my homework in California?" I asked him. Since the beginning of school we had spent the evenings doing our assignments together, even though we were a grade apart.

"You don't need anybody's help." He held my hand in his and stared into my eyes. "You *are* going to write me, aren't you?"

I squeezed his hand. "You know I am. You'd better write to me."

He smiled. As we stared at each other, I knew there was so much we weren't saying. We both knew we'd probably never see each other again. He would go to the prom without me, graduate without me, and marry without me. I couldn't let him see me cry. He cupped the side of my face with his hand.

"Diane," Mother called from the front door. "This red box in your bedroom, are you sending it on the truck or taking it with you?"

"It can go on the truck," I said, my eyes never leaving John's.

Soon, the movers bolted the back doors of the truck and started its big engine. As it drove away, we knew the end was closing in on us.

My dad shut the trunk of the car. "Diane, it's time to go."

"Don't forget me," John pleaded.

I smiled, tears threatening in the corners of my eyes. "Of course not. Nor you me." I took a deep breath. We hugged. Mrs. Greenwalt came to see us off. She hugged me, too.

I watched and waved out the back window as we drove away. Silently, the tears flowed freely. I had been happy here.

*****

Catherine turned and grabbed her daughter's hand. Diane hadn't uttered a sound, but the sight of her tears broke Catherine's heart.

"Honey, you're crying!" Catherine wished she was in the back seat so she could wrap her arms around her daughter and tell her everything was going to work out. Instead, she squeezed Diane's hand. "It's going to be okay. You can write and send pictures or postcards of California. All your friends will want to hear what it's like."

Francis reached and squeezed Diane's ticklish spot above her knee. "What's wrong, Gizmo?" She laughed through tears and pushed his hand away. "You'll love it on the west coast," he reasoned. "We'll go to the beach, Disneyland, and maybe even see some movie stars."

Catherine stared at him and he winked at her. He really didn't comprehend Diane's distress. Still, he thought he was doing what was best for them. Perhaps, he was doing all he knew how to do: move again, always thinking the grass was greener on the other side. But, once there, he'd find out it was only as green as he made it.

*****

They were three days into their journey, having stayed two nights in Mountain Grove to give Catherine a chance to tell her sisters goodbye. She cried when she hugged Essie, and Diane cried when she hugged her grandmother and grandfather. Catherine knew Francis's relationship with his father and mother had greatly improved in the last five years with Francis playing the guitar for their quartet and helping them record some songs. As she watched him hug each of his parents, she thought about how time was not promised and hoped he'd get to see them again. For sure, it wouldn't be as easy to return home from the west coast.

A few hours ago, they left the panhandle of Texas and entered the flatlands of New Mexico. Looking out the window at the vast land, Catherine thought about the wagon trains that passed through there with the threat of Indian raids.

"We need gas." Francis pointed ahead to a sign that read "Indian Trading Post." It was a filling station with a gift shop full of souvenirs from New Mexico. He turned to Diane, "Maybe they'll have something in there you'd like."

Catherine helped Diane pick out an Indian maiden doll with a fringed dress and beaded moccasins. Then Diane spied something else.

"Look, Mom. Aren't these bracelets nifty?"

"I think so," Catherine agreed. "And each of those rocks and stones are native to this area."

After Francis paid for the doll and bracelet and they were walking to the car, Diane touched her mother's arm. "Mom, I still can't believe Anne gave me her ruby bracelet. She loved it so much."

Catherine hugged her. "She loved you more. She wanted you to have something to remember her by."

They continued on their long journey. Francis and Diane listened to the World Series between the St. Louis Cardinals and the Boston Red Sox. There had been a game both days of their travel, and it made the time pass more quickly. Today was the seventh game.

"Oh, Dad, we just have to win. We just have to." Diane voiced her excitement from the back seat.

"Bob Gibson's pitching today," he said. "Of course we'll win."

Tensions were high as they listened to the radio broadcast of the game, but when it was over, the Cardinals were champions again, much to Francis's and Diane's satisfaction.

Catherine kept pouring coffee from the thermos into Francis's cup while he drove long hours without stopping. Even though New Mexico and Arizona were barren and dry, the landscape contained a beauty all its own. Catherine respected the stubbornness of the sagebrush and the determination of the cactus flower to flourish there.

It wasn't until they reached the eastern part of California that Francis stopped and rented a motel room. "We can sleep tonight," he told her. "In the morning, we'll only have maybe half a day's drive left."

The next morning, Francis wanted to start early. After driving a good distance, the desert and the sun still beat down on them, surprising Catherine.

"I expected California to be prettier than this," she admitted.

"It is when you get over on the coast."

"Dad, is this where they filmed *Death Valley Days*?" Diane asked, inquiring about the current western TV series.

"I suppose they might, but Death Valley is actually a little north of us," he explained. "Besides, they probably film a lot of it inside a studio." He addressed his next comment to Catherine, "When we get into L.A., I need to get a paper and we need to find a house *today*."

"Do you really think that's possible?" she asked. They had left Missouri without knowing where they'd live when they arrived at their destination.

"I hope so. We need to contact the moving company and let them know where to deliver our things."

Catherine felt a wave of panic. Then she saw the sign—Welcome to San Bernardino. This was the first real sign of civilization they had seen since entering California. The cars split into multiple lanes of traffic, and there were taco stands on almost every corner. It was about eleven o'clock in the morning, and they still had a ways to go. Anticipation weighed heavily. She hoped L.A. was different than San Bernardino's traffic and haze.

"Can we stop and eat lunch?" Diane asked from the back seat. "I'm starving and we didn't have breakfast."

"We'll eat after we find someplace to live," her father answered sternly, leaving no room for discussion.

Catherine knew Diane was hungry. In fact, she was starving herself. She also understood Francis's stubborn insistence to find a home in a short span of time.

About an hour later, they pulled into the outskirts of L.A. Francis stopped and bought a newspaper. He parked the car in the parking lot of a grocery store close to a telephone booth. He was reading the classifieds and circling houses for rent when Diane spoke up.

"Can't we go in the store and buy something to eat?"

Catherine jumped when he lashed out in rage, "No! I don't want to hear any more about it. Just sit back there and be quiet."

After some time, he took some dimes and the newspaper and went to the pay phone. Catherine watched as he deposited coins, talked, made a mark with his pen, hung up, and then started all over again.

"Mom, can't you go in there and buy us something to eat?"

"It probably won't take your father long. We'll just wait." Even though the windows were rolled down, the heat was

stifling for October. Cars stopped at the
intersection when the light turned red. Their
engines roared when the light changed to
green. Trucks shifted through their gears and
car horns sounded.

Catherine had never had a taco, but
the stand across the street advertised them
for five cents. The McDonald's on the other
corner had nineteen-cent hamburgers, but
Catherine only had a nickel. Two and a half
hours later, she decided to take the nickel in
her purse and go inside the market. She
bought Diane a Three Musketeers bar,—that
was all she could afford. She delighted in
seeing her daughter's eyes widen at the sight
of it.

Francis also seemed delighted when
he finally returned to the car. "I found a two-
bedroom house in Lawndale," he told them.
"It's right off the San Diego Freeway, so I
should be able to get to work fairly easily."

"Great!" Catherine replied. She
wasn't as thrilled about the house as she was
at the prospect of finishing the ordeal.

By five o'clock that evening, they
had rented the house on 163rd street in
Lawndale. Francis called the movers and
they would deliver their furniture tomorrow.

Chapter Thirteen

The movers removed the furniture from the truck and filled every available space in their small house with boxes. Catherine unpacked the wardrobe boxes and several others before bedtime.

She would have continued immediately in the morning, but she needed to enroll Diane in school first. She took all the papers the school in Missouri gave her and, leaving Francis asleep, took her daughter to the junior high in Lawndale. Catherine made Diane wait while she met with the principal in her office.

"I'm really sorry, Mrs. Burch, but we don't have anything to match Missouri's program," the young woman, Miss Hernandez, told her. "The most we can offer Diane is an advanced algebra class."

"No, there must be something you can do," Catherine argued. She had feared this. Even though she held out hope that a similar opportunity would be available here, she knew that reality was slim. With two of her sisters and several of her nieces being long-time teachers, and one of her nephews a dean at Marshall University in Virginia, she knew about curriculum differences between states and even between districts.

Catherine looked at Diane through the big glass window that separated the principal's office from the outer office. The thirteen-year-old sat patiently, her blonde hair straight and long. She was well aware of the opportunity her daughter had lost in this move. She swallowed hard and sighed, "Well, if you can put her in an advanced algebra class, math is her favorite subject." She stood and extended her hand to Miss Hernandez. Before leaving, she kissed Diane and left her to start, once again, as the new kid in school.

*****

I wasn't really nervous on my first day of school in Los Angeles. I couldn't believe how different it was from any school I'd ever attended. There were no hallways, only covered walkways that extended the length of the classrooms. For recreation, I noticed baseball diamonds, but mostly the grounds consisted of basketball courts—at least a dozen of them. Many of the girls wore white lipstick, mini-skirts, and go-go boots. I didn't have white lipstick, but I did have go-go boots; Mom could make any kind of skirt I needed. If I told her about the lipstick, she could probably figure out a way to get that, too.

Most of the students were well-behaved, except for one group of unruly girls. They not only roamed about the classrooms, but all about the school as well, and none of the teachers stopped them.

Thankful for lunchtime, I eagerly followed the crowd toward the cafeteria and got in line. A sign with the menu announced enchiladas for lunch along with rice and refried beans. I didn't know what any of that was. As I waited, I noticed the same unruly girls, about ten of them in all, approaching others in line. They were demanding money and the students were handing it over to them without question! One of them, a blonde with coarse teased hair, approached me. She wasn't smiling and something told me she didn't want to be friends.

"Your lunch money—give it," she demanded, staring at me with dark, cold eyes.

I couldn't comprehend this bizarre behavior. *Was she going to punch me?* Where I came from, girls didn't fight. My stomach growled. "No," I responded emphatically. "It's *my* lunch money and I'm going to eat with it." I saw something change in her eyes. My hands began to tremble, but I wasn't backing down. Hunger became my driving force and I intended to eat!

Neither of us moved. Then, to my surprise, she turned to the girl right after me and extorted her lunch money with a single demand. I should have cared about the person behind me, but, unfortunately, my sudden relief left me numb.

When I finally reached the food, my heart sank. The enchiladas, rice, and refried beans looked like slop for the hogs! I couldn't eat that! Luckily, they did offer a hamburger for the occasional person like me who didn't eat Mexican food.

A girl with short dark hair sat down beside me. "I can't believe you stood up to Charlie," she said and stuffed a bite of slop into her mouth. "That was so groovy. I'm Jamie."

"I'm Diane," I said, before taking a bite of my American hamburger.

"I know," she laughed. "You're in my English class."

Jamie and I became good friends. She feared the girls might retaliate. I wasn't sure what to think.

Academically, my new school wasn't the least bit challenging. However, the social aspect of this gang of girls, thugs in their own right, shocked me. Who at home would believe it? I couldn't wait to write Anne and John!

Los Angeles wasn't at all what I expected. So much concrete existed with very little evidence of grass. We lived on a court and only two houses away from the busy San Diego Freeway. Traffic roared by, except for rush hour when all the lanes were filled with bumper-to-bumper cars and honking horns. We had a very small front yard with some grass, but the rest of the surface was driveway and concrete slab. My bicycle remained in the utility room because the street traffic made it unsafe to ride.

One day while I was walking to school, I noticed a familiar blonde with coarse, teased hair walking down 162nd Street, practically on a collision course with me. I thought about slowing down, but what the heck.

"Diane, isn't it?" she called out. Still no smile.

I nodded, but didn't say anything.

"I didn't know you lived around here," she said as she turned and fell into step beside me.

"Yeah. You, too?" I asked, not exactly sure where this conversation was going.

"Yeah, right there." She turned and pointed to a small house on 162nd Street. I was pretty sure it was behind mine—well, behind the house that was behind mine. Each lot had two houses on them, one in the front and one in the back. They were all jam-packed like sardines. She lived only one street over, but there were actually two houses between the two of ours: the one behind mine and the one behind hers. I never shared with her the exact location of my house.

We continued to make small talk all the way to school. She was as different from me as night and day. She never played softball with the neighborhood kids at the nearest empty field, because there wasn't one. She never let the wind rake through her hair while riding a bicycle like a free spirit, since the busy streets made it impossible to ride. In fact, she had never ridden a bike at all. Her mother worked late and always had men over. Charlie had tough skin because she needed it and smoked for much the same reason.

As we talked, she finally smiled and relaxed some. We would only walk together a few times that entire year, but I could tell Charlie liked me. I'm afraid the same couldn't be said for the rest of her gang.

*****

The mailman delivered two letters today. Catherine opened the one from Larry first. He had been on a ship in Saigon. They'd written each other often, but she worried about him and couldn't wait to hear how he was doing. She read even better news than she expected. His ship would be in San Diego soon and he wanted to come for a visit when he got leave.

Then, she opened the one from Audrey. Audrey explained that they, too, were coming to California. Since Mike's mother lived in San Diego, they were coming in November to visit his mom, and they would be stopping by Lawndale as well.

Catherine clutched the letters close to her heart. She had thought she wouldn't be able to see any of her children after moving so far away. How wonderful! She hadn't seen Larry in—well too long. She couldn't wait to tell Francis when he awoke. She hummed as she cleaned the kitchen and started a pot of coffee.

Sitting with a cup at the table in front of the kitchen window, Catherine realized Francis was right. The sun always shone in California. One couldn't ask for better weather. Perhaps she could enjoy it more if there wasn't so much traffic or the constant whir of cars on the San Diego Freeway, not even a hundred feet from their front door.

Francis liked his job at Northrup. He said the worst part was driving in the traffic. He again worked the second shift. That meant he only saw Diane on the weekends. They still hadn't been to the beach, or much of anywhere.

In the evenings, Catherine and Diane enjoyed watching TV shows like *Laugh-In*, *The Guns of Will Sonnet*, and *The High Chaparral* on their black and white TV.

Catherine had met most of their neighbors. The young couple on the corner had a toddler and wanted Diane to babysit. The family behind them had three girls, and they, too, were looking for an occasional babysitter.

Since moving here, Diane seemed different—withdrawn and moody. Maybe seeing her brother and sister would lift her spirits, like the letter from Anne had yesterday. It was short-lived, though, as she soon retreated to her bedroom. Diane spent a lot of time reading books lately, which wasn't necessarily a bad thing.

When Francis woke up, Catherine wasted no time in sharing the news from the letters with him. He took a coffee cup and filled it from the percolator. "Well, maybe we can see some sights while they're here," he suggested.

Catherine's heart soared. "I'd like that. We haven't been able to see much yet."

"Did Larry's letter say when he thought he'd get leave?"

"No, but his ship is due in Port by the end of November."

Catherine's head spun with thoughts. After Francis left for work, she searched her closet for what she might wear. He'd always bought himself new clothes because he worked, but she'd never known the luxury of new clothes for herself. Occasionally, her children would send her something nice for her birthday, Mother's Day, or Christmas. While raking through the sad state of her wardrobe, she glanced at her right hand where the only diamond she had ever owned rested. Larry sent it to her from Japan.

As it turned out, Mike and Audrey arrived the first of November. Francis took them to see Beverly Hills and the beach. Unfortunately, Diane was in school and not able to go, but that allowed Catherine to enjoy herself with just the four of them.

*****

I hadn't seen my brother in three years. His tour with the Navy took him many places. He sent me souvenirs including a kimono from Japan and a grass skirt from Hawaii.

His plane took off from San Diego about an hour ago, and he'd be here any minute. I couldn't wait. Hearing a noise, I ran to the window and lifted the curtain. A taxi stopped in front of our house. Larry stepped out tall, slender, and proud with his dark blue sailor suit, white hat and duffle bag.

"Mom," I yelled, "he's here!" I heard Mother running from the bedroom. We opened the door and met him outside. There wasn't enough of Larry for us both to hug, but we wrapped ourselves around him anyway.

The last eight weeks had been hard, but I didn't want to think about that. Instead, my brother, who I teased as a child, who gave me go kart rides and took me into the swamp in a pirogue, was home.

165

We laughed and talked through dinner, just the three of us. Dad was at work and would see Larry tomorrow morning. Mom made more coffee while he played his harmonica and I played the guitar, showing him my improvement.

That night, Mom and Larry made a makeshift bed in the living room. After she went to sleep, he and I lay there talking. He told me about his travels. I noticed his tattoos and increased cigarette smoking, definite traits of being a sailor. We talked about his old girlfriends and the Japanese girl who stole his heart.

I told him only about my life before moving here—before the horrible existence of living in L.A. and that awful gang of girls who harassed everyone at school and beyond. I also chose not to mention how Dad didn't come home sometimes on the weekends. I didn't tell him that at night, I could hear Mother crying in her bed. On Monday, I walked to school and Larry left to go back to the Navy.

According to the song, *"If you were going to San Francisco, you were going to meet some gentle people there."* You could wear flowers in your hair and run through the park with the sun shining above and the wind in your face. California, home of the long-haired hippies, flower girls, and "sittin' on the dock of the bay," was suggestive of beauty, peace, love-ins, and happiness. I found it to be anything but. Gone were my dreams of the beach at sunset and movie stars. I yearned for all I had lost and all I left behind in Missouri.

I sought that elusive beauty and peace in the pages of books. I had read all sorts before, like *Black Beauty*, *Charlotte's Web*, and others, but this year, at the age of thir-teen, I found romance and refuge in their pages. The Bible I had received for memorizing the 23rd *Psalm* sat on my dres-ser collecting dust while I lived in the written adventures of heroines in far-off lands. Detailed histories surrounding exci-ting plots and rich characters absorbed me.

Christmas would be here soon. I had been babysitting and earned a little bit of money. I'm not sure why, but not until this year did I realize that in Christmases past, Dad didn't buy Mom presents. Even her birthday seemed to come and go without recognition. This Christmas, I wanted to buy Mom something special, something new and pretty. My mother was pretty and she should have pretty things. She should have a husband who stood beside her.

I walked down Hawthorne Boulevard, looking in the stores for a special gift. I came upon a pair of gold dangly earrings. They were diamond shaped and louvered, quite stylish, and they were clip-on. Mom didn't have pierced ears. I didn't have enough money to buy them yet, but after babysitting this weekend, I could come back. They were perfect.

We put up a Christmas tree and hung the same shiny, precious ornaments on it. I wrapped Mom's earrings and put them under the tree. Somehow, it didn't feel like Christmas without snow; the temperatures still soared in the eighties.

I awoke on Christmas morning to find that Dad had not come home. Still, Mom had my stocking laid out and stuffed. She sat beside me, putting her arm around me while I dug out the goodies she had stuffed inside. They were little things she had picked up over the weeks with ten cents here and fifteen there, all on change she found over time under the cushions of the sofa.

There was a bottle of nail polish, finger nail file and clippers, some white lipstick, my favorite candy, and a little bottle of perfume. I had wanted all these things and was overjoyed at receiving them.

"I'm sorry, it's not much," she apologized.

"Oh, Mom," I hugged her. "I think it's the best Christmas ever."

I watched as she opened her earrings. Her eyes lit up. "Put them on," I said.

They looked good on her and gave her a modern look as they dangled with her every movement. The only stylish shirt Mother owned was a green paisley print, so

she put it on to match. Dad came home a
little later.

Chapter Fourteen
January 1968

It didn't matter what Catherine said, Francis was insistent he move into an apartment closer to his work. "The traffic robs my time and wears me out," he reasoned. "I can rest and concentrate on work. I'll come home on the weekends."

When she realized she couldn't stop him, she decided to test the situation. "Well, okay, I'll go with you and we'll look at apartments."

"That's not necessary," he said too quickly. "I've already found one in San Pedro."

Catherine felt a knife pierce her heart. "Well, I'll help you get it ready," she offered, but he interrupted her.

"It's already furnished."

She watched him neatly fold and carefully pack his pants, shirts, handkerchiefs, and socks into a suitcase. Her back had ached when she meticulously washed and ironed those pants, shirts, and handkerchiefs so her husband would look his best for his job.

Just before leaving for his shift, he awkwardly kissed her. "Goodbye, Kid," he said with a look in his eyes she didn't recognize.

As she watched him drive away, a tear rolled down her cheek. She felt tired, very tired. Maybe she could take a nap before Diane came home from school.

The next two weeks, Francis didn't return. The second Wednesday, a representtative from the gas company knocked on the door. The bill hadn't been paid. Catherine had no money so they shut off the gas, thus rendering the kitchen stove worthless and reducing Diane and her to taking cold showers.

"Mom, why wouldn't Dad pay the bill?" Diane asked.

"I don't know, Honey."

"Why did he have to move into an apartment?"

"Well, to be closer to his work," Catherine managed before she quickly picked up their dishes and turned toward the sink so Diane couldn't see the tears stinging her eyes.

Catherine used the electric skillet to cook and the percolator to warm water, but many uncertainties nagged at her. Without a telephone, she had no way to contact him. She didn't even have an address for the apartment. Now that the gas had been shut off, would the electricity and water be next? What about the rent? Would she and Diane eventually be on the street homeless?

Catherine had never worked a day in her life. Without a car, what in the world could she possibly do?

That night she cried as she prayed with her heart completely broken. She didn't feel worthy to receive an answer, but she still asked God to show her the way.

After Diane left for school the next morning, Barbara Anderson, the next door neighbor, knocked on the door. She carried her four-week-old baby girl in her arms.

"Oh," Catherine smiled and opened the screen door, "I'm so glad you're here. I've been wanting to see this precious little one."

It felt natural as she tenderly held the baby. She had seven babies of her own and missed caring for a little one.

"You know," Barbara told her, "with three children, it's much harder than I realized. I'm not sure what I'm going to do when I go back to work."

"What do you mean?"

"Well, I have to get three kids fed and dressed, pack a diaper bag, and drive thirty minutes out of my way before I can even think about heading to work."

"Bless your heart. I can't imagine," Catherine empathized, but Barbara said she had an idea.

"I was hoping, Catherine, that I could talk you into babysitting," she announced. "I would pay you well. If you could come over in the mornings, feed and dress the kids, then watch them at my house, it would make my life much easier."

"Why, sure," Catherine said. "I'd love to."

After Mrs. Anderson left, Catherine closed the door, leaned against it, and looked toward the ceiling. "Thank you," she uttered to an unseen God, thankful for His help.

That Saturday, Francis came home. When Catherine told him about the gas being turned off, he had an excuse.

"I forgot, but I've taken care of it. Monday, they should turn it back on," he explained.

Then she reminded him, "So, I thought you were coming home on the weekends."

"Well, I had to work overtime and there was no way to let you know."

His story made sense, but it didn't remove all her fears. "Maybe it's time for us to get a telephone again."

"You know we can't do that," he objected. "The minute I get a telephone, Leo and his thugs will find us."

"Francis, it's been eight years. You don't honestly think he's still looking, do you?" she argued.

"You never know. Anyway, the phone company will want to collect that big car lot bill we left unpaid. We can't afford that right now."

"You know, I bet I can get it in my name and they'll never connect the two." It made perfect sense to Catherine, who realized they really needed a means of communication if they were to have two residences. "What if I have an emergency?"

"Well, you can call work, I suppose, but only if it's a real emergency. They probably won't like it."

She watched him play music with Diane. He even took his usual spot on the sofa and watched *Perry Mason* that afternoon. On the surface, he appeared the dutiful husband and father, but why couldn't she believe it?

When darkness fell and Diane finally went to bed, Catherine went to their bedroom. She didn't know if Francis would stay in the living room watching television or if he would come to bed. She donned her ragged nightgown and climbed between the sheets.

She heard Francis enter the room and remove his shirt and then his pants. He folded his pants neatly and draped them over the chair. She felt his weight on his side of the bed. He pulled her into his arms and tugged at her nightgown.

"What are you doing?" she asked. But, she knew he was removing the last bit of cloth separating the two of them. She should be happy; this was what she wanted: for him to come home, make love to her, and tell her she was the only one for him. She had to shake off this feeling. He was her husband and she his wife.

Afterward, they lay naked. "I have to go to the bathroom." She pointed to his side of the room, "Hand me my nightgown."

"Why? You don't need it."

"Francis, I don't have any clothes on."

"I know." He laughed and ran his fingers over the swell of her breast and down her abdomen. "You're just walking down the hall. Go on and I'll watch."

"Francis, don't be ridiculous. Diane's in the next room. I can't go parading about naked."

He sighed. "You're such a killjoy," he said and handed her the nightgown.

He fell asleep in the next few minutes while she lay awake and pondered her situation. All of her feminine confidence evaporated. She couldn't possibly parade her fifty-five-year-old body in front of her forty-two-year-old husband.

Catherine hoped Francis was going through a phase, hoped that all he had told her about his disappearance was truthful. Unfortunately, he left on Monday and afterward only returned very infrequently, always with some story that seemed to explain his absence. She was torn.

Catherine babysat for four weeks and saved her earnings. She used Barbara's telephone to call the company and request a telephone in the name of Catherine Burch. She smiled at Diane's excitement when they installed it.

"Can I give the number to my friends?" Diane asked. "Can they call me?"

"Of course," Catherine told her. "You can even call Grandma and Grandpa."

"Really? But that's long distance."

Catherine laughed. "Well, don't talk too long."

*****

March 1968

During free time at school, we mostly played basketball. If John could only be here, I would kiss him for teaching me to shoot. I proved to be real competition for all those California girls who'd been playing most of their lives. I enjoyed the game and made a few friends in the process. In particular, a tall girl, Teresa, and I often took on a team for a little two-on-two.

As news of the upcoming election spread, I began to think about the presidential candidates. Bobby Kennedy had my vote, if I could only vote. I heard about civil rights and racial riots in the South, but I didn't really know what to think. I remembered Kansas City and the black people who rode at the back of the bus. I didn't know what the big deal was. They could've sat next to me. I didn't understand why we couldn't all live together harmoniously. Dr. Martin Luther King became a familiar name.

Stories of the war in Vietnam led every newscast. If you were male and a teenager, you could pretty much bank on being drafted. Young people protested, but I believed, hard as it might be, one should serve their country when called. It was the patriotic thing to do.

Our neighbor, Eileen, and her husband, Paul, lived in the curve of our cul-de-sac in the rear house. One night, they invited us over for dinner, just Mom and me. We hadn't seen Dad in a while. Besides, he'd be working anyway. I put on my best clothes, but Mom didn't have very much. She wore her green paisley shirt and pants again.

We rang the doorbell. Eileen, who was from England, answered the door and spoke in her lovely British accent, "Hello, come on in."

Mother handed her a bowl covered with a tea towel. "I brought some yeast rolls."

"They smell absolutely delicious, Catherine."

As we entered, I noticed dishes sat elegantly in place on the table and all four places included wine glasses. Eileen and Paul treated us like guests of honor. I watched Mom, who looked happy talking to them. She had been so sad recently.

"I have wine to accompany our meal," Eileen explained, "but I didn't know if you wanted Diane to have any or not."

Mom thought for a moment while I entreated. "I suppose she could have one small glass just to taste."

After eating, we all watched *The High Chaparral* on their color television.

Eileen sold a nice line of clothes, but not in stores. Before the night ended, she brought out several stylish dresses, blouses, and slacks, all in Mom's size. I watched Mom finger the materials.

"No, I probably shouldn't," she said.

"Mom, try this one on." It was a matching top and skirt of peach trimmed in ivory. The polyester and cotton knit was buttery smooth.

"No, I can't afford this."

"Please," I coaxed, "Just try it on."

When Mother walked out in the nicest dress she had ever donned, it transformed her. She appeared slimmer and even her face glowed. Eileen and I prodded her into trying on several pieces, all of which made Mother look younger and decreased her sorrowful shadows.

Eileen gave mother a discount and before we left, Mom bought three outfits. I couldn't have been happier, even if they were for me.

*****

Catherine loved babysitting the Andersons' children. The three of them were no trouble at all, and Barbara did indeed pay her well. Francis seldom came home anymore, and she was thankful to have money to buy groceries for her and Diane. The two of them would walk ten blocks to the market and ten blocks back, carrying brown paper bags of food.

The winter months had come and gone without any cold weather. However, on April 5, someone knocked on the door as Catherine was watching a special news report on the assassination of Dr. Martin Luther King, Jr. She didn't answer until Walter Cronkite finished his sentence. Through the screen she saw the man whose shirt was embroidered with the electric company emblem.

"May I help you?" she asked.

The man stared at his clipboard. "Are you Mrs. Burch?"

"Yes, I am."

"Well, Ma'am, your bill of $53.78 hasn't been paid. Unless you can pay that now, I'll have to shut off the electricity." He glanced at her briefly before looking back down.

"Yes, I can pay that now," she told him. So Francis hadn't paid the electric bill. Luckily, she had about seventy-five dollars in her purse. She paid the man and he wrote her a receipt.

She hadn't seen Francis for several weeks now. It bothered her most at night, after Diane went to bed and all was quiet. She tried not to think about him—where he was, what he was doing—but failed miserably. In the beginning, she could tell herself he was working overtime and would be home soon, but now she knew better.

Diane had told her about a gang of girls at school who bullied and took money from the students. "I'd rather they'd rub my face in the dirt than surrender to their demands," her daughter told her.

The other day during P.E. class, Diane and one of the girls actually got into a fight. Apparently Diane prevailed, while the other girls in the gang only watched. Catherine knew her daughter was concerned about them retaliating. Jamie, Diane's friend, said the girls carried knives.

These were the types of things about which she wanted to talk with Francis. He would want to know if Diane was in danger. *Why doesn't he come home?* She cried when she thought about her life. She had loved Kenneth, but he had abandoned her. Now, it was happening all over again with Francis. She knew the chances that work was what kept him away were slim. The thought of him with someone else, perhaps younger, sickened her.

Catherine kept all her thoughts inside. Even though she had a telephone, she couldn't call any of her children because, although they might not say it, they'd think, "I told you so." Not that they wouldn't care—she knew they would—but more than that, Catherine didn't want them to believe the worst about Francis. She couldn't call Essie or any of her siblings for the same reasons. She felt utterly alone. *Please God, this just has to be a phase he's going through. Let it be over soon,* she thought.

In spite of his recent behavior, Catherine still loved him. She remembered their early years: his tenderness when she was pregnant, how much he missed her when he was in Seattle, and his passion in New Orleans. But the last few years had taken their toll. She wasn't getting any younger, and he seemed younger than ever.

She heard the front door as Diane arrived home from school, wearing a frown.

"Sorry, I'm late. Teresa made Anna mad at her today and she was afraid to walk home by herself. She begged me to walk her home!"

"Is Anna in that gang?"

"Yeah. I'm not sure what Teresa thought I could do. I can't help but look over my shoulder all the time. I wish we'd never moved here!"

She stomped off to her bedroom and didn't hear Catherine's soft reply, "Me, too."

*****

In my bedroom, I turned on my transistor radio. Bobby Goldsboro was singing *Honey*. Usually, when he got to the part about missing her and being good I always cried anyway, but now I stretched out on my bed and sobbed. *Why do I have to live here? I don't like being scared—scared to go to school, scared to walk home. It's not right. Because Dad works in the aerospace industry, we always move around, but why couldn't we have stayed in O'Fallon? And where are you, Dad? I really miss you.*

I struggled to gain my composure and wipe the tears away. I knew I had to stop crying because Mother was having a hard enough time. Every night I heard her sniffling.

I noticed my Bible sitting on my dresser. I hardly ever looked at it, but I could feel the presence of God in this turmoil. I picked it up and blew the dust off. I started reading in *Matthew*. I didn't always understand the words, but they were comforting.

In the midst of a gang-infested Los Angeles and the impending divorce of my parents, I decided to take a walk and escape to the "nature" path of concrete and filth alongside the San Diego Freeway next to our house. The sun hung low in the sky. The only barrier between me and the cars that endlessly whizzed by was a chain link fence.

Carbon monoxide fumes flooded the air. I replayed the fight I had with one of the girls of that relentless gang.

I longed for the simpler days of baseball, apple pie, and the St. Louis Cardinals. As my heart sank, I decided to look into the hazy sky and talk to my best friend—the One who never left my side, the One who promised to never leave me or forsake me.

Instead of focusing on my troubles, I thanked God for my ears that could hear when others couldn't. I thanked Him for my eyes that could see. Even though my sight was less than perfect, at least I could see when others weren't as fortunate. I thanked Him for my legs and arms and for my mind; the list went on and on. Never had I felt this good. Praising God and thanking Him made my problems seem smaller. He might not take them away, but I knew He would help me get through them. God was showing me how important it was to pray.

That next day, Saturday, Dad came home. This made Mother happier. Dad and I played music, and he watched westerns on television.

Sunday morning, I awoke to the sound of Mom whispering in my ear. "Wake up, Diane. I thought we'd go to church this morning."

I rubbed my eyes, trying to open them. "What?" I couldn't believe my ears!

This would be the first time Mother and I ever attended church without being at my grandparents' house. I dressed quickly. Mother wore her new peach outfit. She looked nice. We left Dad sleeping and drove the car to a little church about two miles away.

I enjoyed the singing and sat quietly next to Mother during the sermon. At the end, when they sang "I Surrender All," Mother left me and walked down the aisle to the altar, handkerchief in hand. I watched her cry and talk to the preacher who took her hand in his. They knelt and prayed.

*****

"How can I help you, my child?" the preacher asked as he took Catherine's hand in his.

"I fear I'm not worthy," she managed to say through tears.

"All have sinned and fallen short of the glory of God," he replied. "Have you trusted Jesus as your savior?"

"Many years ago. But since then, I'm afraid I haven't always been as I should."

"If we confess our sins, he is faithful and just to forgive us of our sins and to cleanse us from all unrighteousness."

"Yes. I need Him to show me the way. My husband and I..." she couldn't finish. The seasoned man of God nodded, and together they knelt.

Her tears flowed freely. She couldn't stop them and she could no longer speak.

She heard the preacher begin praying. "Show her the way, Lord. May your will be done in her life and in her home."

When she walked back to Diane, she possessed a new strength. Although her eyes were still moist, she could still see her daughter's concern. Afterward, they drove home together in silence and peace.

When they walked inside, Francis was awake and playing the guitar. He took notice of her peach suit, glancing from her neck to her heels. She could feel the warmth in her face.

"Where'd you guys go?" he asked.

She took her gloves off and placed them and her purse on the table. "We went to church."

He raised his eyebrows and nodded as he played a familiar melody, "The Tennessee Waltz." That brought back memories. Did he remember their first dance was to that song? She smiled and swayed to the music in front of him.

"Your Dad and I danced to this song before you were born," she explained to Diane, watching his face for any sign of recognition. With a blank look, he stared at her above his guitar while strumming.

"You don't remember?"

His eyes met hers. "I remember."

Francis turned to Diane. "Play along with me."

"I don't know it."

"I'll teach you."

A wonderful joy filled Catherine's heart. Having Francis at home and interacting with them pleased her. She went to the bedroom to change clothes before cooking lunch. The three of them sat at the table and ate. She watched Francis talk with Diane. She loved him for all of his abilities and admired him for his accomplishments. After all, he had helped to build space capsules that orbited the moon. She loved him enough to wait for this phase to pass.

The next afternoon, Francis left for work and her happiness slowly dissipated as weeks again went by without a word from him.

*****

May 1968

The school year in California wouldn't be over until the middle of June. I couldn't wait. It had been a long year. One day in May, the 3:30 school bell rang. I gathered my books and talked with Jamie for a while before I began walking. I had almost made it home when up ahead I noticed a crowd of junior high students surrounding something. They were jeering and acting weirdly. I couldn't see what was happening. As I drew closer, crazy laughter rang out from those closest to the center. I tried to see what all the fuss was about. My stomach started tying in knots. The kids in front of me shifted slightly, allowing me to catch sight of a young girl, about my age, in the middle.

I recognized the gang of boys who were snickering and taunting her. I saw the terror in her eyes. Then I noticed her dress had been ripped at the shoulder, exposing her slip and bra strap. I wanted to scream, kick, hit, and maybe even kill. I HAD HAD IT HERE! Without even realizing it, I advanced forward as strength rose within me. I pushed and shoved my way through the crowd, grabbed the girl's arm, and pulled her through the people.

I don't remember if anyone said anything to me. I didn't care. I don't know if they followed us. We actually ran the rest of the way to my house without looking back.

"Mom," I hollered as we ran inside. "This is…" I stopped and looked at the girl with dark hair and tears. "I don't know your name." I was out of breath and my voice was high. I sensed that Mother instantly knew something was wrong.

"Julie," the girl said with wild eyes.

"What's happened?" Mother asked.

I answered with words that came too quickly, and my whole body began to shake. "These boys—they ripped her dress. Can you help her, Mom?"

"Julie," Mother said, "call your house and tell your parents where you are. I'll get a needle and thread and see what I can do with your dress." She left the room.

I could see Julie was too upset to talk to anybody. I picked up the phone. "What's your number?" I asked. After I told Julie's mother where I lived, she began to calm down. While we waited, the two of us talked. She was telling me she had just moved here from Fort Worth, Texas, when Mother came back with needle in hand.

"Oh, really! Two of Diane's sisters live in Fort Worth." She quickly mended Julie's dress before her mom arrived to get her.

Afterward, I couldn't stop shaking. I realized what I had done. I had gone against perhaps the strongest gang in my school. That night, I prayed and asked God to protect me. I couldn't remember a time when I had been this unhappy. I missed my friends, I missed Missouri, and I missed my dad.

When I arrived at school, no one approached me, and I didn't receive any bad glares from anyone. All appeared fine.

On June 4th, I was looking forward to the end of school, which was in just a few days. The news never really interested me much, but because of this year's presidential election, I had paid attention. In my thirteen-year-old mind, I still believed the right candidate for the nation was Robert F. Kennedy. Surely, he would win. That night, he won the California primary. After his acceptance speech in Los Angeles and sometime after midnight, a man named Sirhan Sirhan shot him in the head. For the next twenty-six hours I prayed for Bobby to live, but on June 6th, he died. I cried for his wife who was expecting her tenth child. I cried for a family who had lost three sons as they served their country.

Chapter Fifteen
June 1968

Catherine read the letter again. Essie wrote about a spring of rain. They expected a good crop of tomatoes, corn, cucumbers, green beans, and melons. Essie, Mag, and Ola planned to get together soon to can strawberry, blackberry, and raspberry preserves. Jim was running about 100 head of cattle on the pasture with a good number of milk cows. Audrey, Mike, and the boys had been down over the weekend. Genevieve drove over to get the boys, dressed in her classy black dress and pearls.

Catherine missed the green Ozark hills in springtime and early summer. What a contrast to the smoggy skies of L.A. How she wished she could feel the dirt between her fingers while working in the garden. She remembered years of canning fresh fruits and vegetables. She smiled at the part about Genevieve, her grandsons' other grandmother, because she remembered complimenting Genevieve years ago on always looking nice. The woman had told her, "Every woman should have one black dress in her wardrobe and a set of pearls in her box."

Catherine noticed their red Mercury drive up outside. Francis walked to the door. Quickly, she folded the letter and ran to the bedroom to brush her hair. She heard the front door open as she ran the tube of lipstick over her lips. Thank God she wasn't wearing her housecoat, but had gotten dressed into the pantsuit she bought from Eileen.

"Daddy!" Diane hollered and ran to hug him.

"Hi, Gizmo." He winked and made a clicking sound with his mouth.

"We never know when you're going to show up," Catherine said as she entered the living room. She approached her husband to kiss him hello. He gave her an awkward peck on the lips.

"I thought I'd take Gizmo, here, for a drive." He turned to Diane, "You want to go for a drive?"

"Sure. Where are we going?"

"You'll see."

"Let me freshen up." Diane left for the bathroom, but called over her shoulder. "You going, too, Mom?"

Catherine looked at Francis. Something wasn't right. His eyes didn't meet hers. It was Saturday, and even though he hadn't been home in a while, usually when he arrived on a Saturday, he behaved differently.

"I thought maybe I should spend some time with Diane," he explained. "You don't mind, do you?"

Catherine shook her head. "No, I think that's a good idea." She wanted to tell him how much she missed him. How she wished the two of them could be alone together, take a drive just him and her, explain to him how she was dying inside, convince him to stop whatever it he was doing and return home.

When Diane came out of her room, she beamed with excitement. Catherine hoped the two of them would have a good time. She watched them leave through the living room window with a sinking feeling inside, a feeling of sadness and doom.

*****

We had lived in California almost a year, but I hadn't seen Dad much because he seldom ever came home. He had an apartment close to his work and sometimes wouldn't come home for several weeks.

I'm not sure what Mother thought about Dad wanting to take me for a drive. I couldn't have been happier. Since we only owned one car and he always had it with him, I jumped at the chance to go anywhere. But this was special; he wanted to spend time alone with me. We drove through the congested boulevards of Los Angeles. I looked at him and smiled when he smiled.

We passed through light after light before turning into the parking lot of a little café.

The hostess seated us in a booth by the window. I felt all grown-up and important sitting there with my father. I had missed the man who taught me to play the guitar and how to throw a baseball. Today, it felt great spending time with him and knowing *he* wanted to spend time with *me*.

It was awkward at first. I didn't know what to say.

"So what are you going to order?" he asked when the waitress came back. Didn't he know?

"I'll have a hamburger, fries, and a chocolate shake," I told her. I always ordered this. He requested a roast beef sandwich and a cup of coffee. We talked a little while we ate, but Dad seemed nervous and kept looking out the window as if he were watching for something.

I slurped my shake, getting the last drop from the bottom of the glass. Then the bell jingled and the door opened. I watched this lady with deep black hair puffed up in a bee hive walk in and twist over to our table. Even stranger still, Dad quickly scooted over and she sat down beside him.

"Diane," he said to me with a twinkle in his eye, "I want you to meet Mary." He practically spilled his coffee with giddiness. I suddenly realized he intended the twinkle for Mary and not for me!

I simply replied, "Hi," hoping she was a mere acquaintance and would be leaving soon.

Mary's thick, fake eyelashes curled up teasingly. Her fiery-red, long nails matched the color of her lips. She opened her purse, pulled out a cigarette, and put it to her mouth. Jumping like a panting dog chasing a bitch in heat, Dad flicked his lighter and she was lit. They sat goo-goo-eyed at first, then they kissed. I squirmed and tasted the bile at my throat.

He turned to me. "Diane? I met Mary and we just fell in love," he declared. I stared at his lips. If only they had stopped then, but they didn't. They kept moving, spewing out more words—words that should never have been said. "I'm going to leave your mother and marry her."

All the air suddenly left the room. I couldn't breathe. My stomach churned into knots. I felt faint and queasy.

I sat dazed. The bitter sobs of my mother as she cried herself to sleep at night echoed in my ears. I thought about the difficulties of this past year, like when Mom and I had walked to the store because we had no car and then carried home bags of heavy groceries.

"Your father wants you to live with us," Mary was saying.

Dad must have sensed a storm brewing across the table. He asked for the check and we all left. Outside, he hurried to the passenger side of the car to open the door for Mary. Apparently, it was a feat she wouldn't have been able to accomplish on her own.

Once inside the car, the conversation resumed. I feared my inability to control my anger. I realized that all this time I had spent missing my father, needing his love and provision, he had chosen to spend with this …this…woman!

When they pressed me for an answer about my future living arrangements, I turned on Mary, struggling to keep my voice calm. "I've watched my dad light your cigarette, open your car door, and shower you with attention. None of these things does he do for my mother. One day, he won't do them for you either." I had so much more to say.

"Diane," Dad scolded me. "That's a serious thing to say to Mary."

"Excuse me," I snapped. "I thought this was a serious situation." It was the first time I ever talked back to my father. My pulse raced with fright while my heart broke.

Defeated and tight-lipped, Dad dropped me off at home. I watched him and Mary drive away.

That day, I decided I would live with Mom. I never wanted to play the guitar any more—ever.

*****

Catherine heaved over the toilet, losing the little bite she had eaten for lunch. When Diane had told her about Francis and Mary, her belly immediately rolled into a ball of fire. She had barely made it to the bathroom in time.

She doused her face with cold water. It helped, but she still felt like someone had punched her in the stomach. She should cry, scream, kick, or something, but instead, her entire body felt like lead.

When she emerged from the bathroom, Diane was sitting in the living room, staring at her guitar. She decided to ask a few questions. How old was Mary? Was she pretty? Had he actually said he was going to marry her? How could he marry her, when he was still married? Actually, they talked the remainder of the afternoon, discussing the lunch and what was said. Catherine knew Diane hurt. She wished she could make everything all right, but that wasn't within her ability. Her daughter needed her, and all she could do was be there.

When Diane announced she was going to read a book in her room, Catherine welcomed the silence. She sat alone on the couch as the sun set and the light grew dim. She didn't know what to do. Her eyes filled with tears that spilled over onto her cheeks. Minutes passed into hours.

Suddenly, the lamp beside her switched on.

"Listen to this," Diane said. "Listen to what I just read." Diane held her Bible a little closer to her face.

Catherine took the handkerchief from her pocket, dried her face, and blew her nose. "Okay," she answered.

Diane began reading in *Matthew 13:37-39*. Jesus was telling a parable about a man who sowed good seed in his field, but in the night, an enemy came and sowed tares or weeds among the wheat so that as the wheat grew, weeds sprang up amongst it. When Jesus's disciples asked him to explain, "He answered and said unto them, 'He that soweth the good seed is the Son of man; the field is the world, the good seed are the children of the kingdom, but the tares are the children of the wicked one; the enemy that sowed them is the devil; the harvest is the end of the world; and the reapers are the angels.'"

Catherine somehow found comfort in those words, a promise that though the world contained evil and good, ultimately God was victorious in the end. She found a hope for a time where all would be good, a time that never ended. Catherine looked at Diane's teary eyes through tears of her own.

"Oh, Honey, I love that! Would you mind writing it down for me? We'll put it on the refrigerator."

After Diane wrote the scripture on notebook paper, Catherine taped it to the fridge. She read it over and over again during the days that followed, and each time, it reminded her that God had not forsaken her, nor would He.

"In this world you will have trouble. But take heart! I have overcome the world."

John 16:33

*****

Catherine remained seated, even though she saw Francis through the window before he opened the front door. The despicable look on his face caused a lump to form in her throat. Upon seeing him, Diane went outside to play. Only then did he venture to sit in the chair across from her.

"We have to talk," he said softly.

She didn't want to talk, didn't want to hear whatever he had to say.

"You know I haven't been happy for some time," he continued.

He hadn't been happy? *He* hadn't been happy? Well, of course, he would only be thinking about himself. "Why? Why is that?" she countered. "What have I done or not done, except try to make *you* happy?"

He rubbed his face with his fist. "I just don't love you anymore."

"You love her—what's her name—Mary?"

"Yes, I love Mary."

Catherine stared at him with contempt. "Because she's younger."

"No, that's not it."

"You remember you said it was me you wanted; that when I was old, you'd push my wheelchair." She paused as fury mounted within her. "You son-of-a-bitch!"

She shouldn't have said that, but it felt good.

"I meant it. I did." His eyes sought hers. "It's just that we don't have fun anymore...in the bedroom."

"Well, maybe if you were here more, we could."

"No, it doesn't work between us. Mary doesn't need clothes. She'll walk down the hall with nothing on. We're free to be and do what we want."

Catherine shook her head. "Because I'm here taking care of your daughter, keeping food in the icebox, and paying the utility bills. That's what makes you free."

A long silence passed.

"You're willing to walk away from your daughter?"

He sighed. "Of course not. I wanted her to live with me."

At that, as hard as she could, Catherine hurled her glass at him, missing her target by only an inch.

He flinched. "Damn."

"You want a divorce?"

"Yes."

"I will NEVER give you a divorce. I'm your wife and Diane is your daughter. We are your home." She stood and walked into the kitchen. She looked at the sheet of notebook paper taped to the refrigerator. Her hands trembled and she felt sick. The scripture she read soothed her soul. Then, she heard Francis letting himself out the door.

Diane came back inside and wanted to know what he said.

"He doesn't love me anymore." Catherine told her youngest everything. Maybe she shouldn't have, but Diane was all she had and they would stick together through this.

"Mom, Dad doesn't know how to love. *The Bible* says God is love. If Dad doesn't know God, then he doesn't know love."

Catherine felt the comfort of Diane's arms as they hugged her. "Oh, Honey, I don't know what we're going to do," she admitted. "God will have to show us."

*****

It was five o'clock in the morning when Catherine abandoned trying to sleep. She prepared a pot of coffee. With her cup in hand, she sat down in the living room. The phone rested on the end table beside the sofa. She stared at it, dreading what she must do. The cold stillness of the night held her hostage. She'd contemplated every possible scenario, and now as the sun came up, it was time. Five o'clock here meant seven o'clock in Texas. She picked up the phone and slowly dialed the numbers, pushing her middle finger through each hole, sliding it clockwise and then releasing, letting the dial ratchet its way back to its place.

Had the journey she started on fourteen years ago really come to an end? Was this it? She still held onto a diminishing hope that her husband would see the error in his ways and remember he loved her.

Nevertheless, it was time to seek help. Wallace and Audrey both lived in Illinois, but calling Wallace was unthankable. Audrey would want to help, but Catherine didn't think that was a good solution either. No, Linda and LouAnn in Texas seemed the better choice. Linda had three children and no extra bedrooms. Buck and Larry were also in Texas, but Buck's house was full and Larry was a bachelor. LouAnn and Billy recently bought a nice home in Bedford, and since they only had Paul and Lori Ann, Catherine decided to call LouAnn.

*****

I helped Mom as we went through every item in the house, deciding if it was to be taken with us, sold in the rummage sale, or left behind. Since we'd be flying, we could only take a few things. Our thoughtful neighbors helped as Mom and I set up our wares, hoping to raise a little money. The tables were filled with items that represented pieces of our lives. Mom sold the Depression glass and special dishes that had belonged to her mother. She sold the sewing machine and anything she thought might bring a good price because we needed the money.

"Should we sell my bicycle?" I asked, willing to do my part.

"No," she said emphatically. "We're not going to sell your bike. We're going to leave it here." I didn't understand, but I didn't argue.

I didn't know whether to be happy or sad, but I felt both at the same time. Finally, I would be leaving California and looking forward to a new school, perhaps more like what I had left in Missouri. As happy as that thought was, my mother's sorrow and the loss of Dad in our lives overshadowed it.

Flying for the first time excited Mom and me. Dad had wanted me to leave my dog, Oscar, because it cost too much for him to fly. Mom said no. She told him I had lost enough already. She wasn't going to let me lose my dog, too. She paid the extra money for the fare.

LouAnn and Mom talked several times over the last few days. LouAnn said they were looking forward to seeing us. She worked as a supervisor at a department store. She'd talked with her boss and he decided to hire mother for a sales position. The job was waiting until she got there.

Dad took us to the airport and we said our goodbyes. He hugged me extra tightly. I didn't cry, not because I didn't have reason, but because I was tired of crying. He kissed Mom, and afterward she told him, "When you come to your senses, you know where I am."

I watched Oscar's cage disappear with our luggage. I entered the Boeing 727, sat in a window seat, and looked outside at the Sky Chef's truck. Then I turned to Mom. "I'm never coming back here, ever," I told her.

"No, I would never make you," she promised.

Chapter Sixteen

The stewardesses on the flight from L.A. to Dallas served the meal, but Catherine couldn't eat a bite. LouAnn and Billy were going to pick them up at Love Field. For financial reasons, she wanted to start work as soon as possible, but the thought made her nervous.

At fifty-five, she'd never had an official job, one from which she could get fired. *What if I can't do it?* she thought. *I've never failed at anything before.* Had she failed at being a wife? Marital contentment proved impervious to trying to be supportive, hardworking, and loving while persevering. She swallowed hard past the lump in her throat and blinked away the tears.

Life opened a new chapter with this flight. Alone and scared, she embraced the unknown. But then, hadn't she already been alone?

That day on the courthouse steps, Kenneth had pleaded, "Let's go back in there and get married again." What if she'd agreed? How might her life be different now? No, she wouldn't allow herself to think about it.

Life hadn't been all bad with Francis. They traveled all over the country, seeing and experiencing more than she ever imagined. They survived bad times as well as good. The two of them had loved each other and longed for each other. Now, to think of him with someone else made her queasy, and it didn't help that she was thirteen and half years older than them both. She glanced out the window at the fluffy, white billows of clouds.

"Isn't it groovy, Mom?"

Catherine nodded. "Absolutely beautiful." Flying for the first time, being up above the world and watching cars and houses become tiny little specks below them, like ants racing about on an ant farm, had been quite an adventure.

The pilot spoke over the speaker system, saying the plane would be landing in Dallas in about thirty minutes. It had taken them two hours and forty-five minutes to fly the same distance it had taken the three of them two and a half days to drive.

The silver lining of moving to Texas was Catherine would be close to five of her children and their families: Linda, LouAnn, Buck, Larry, and Diane, of course. She and Diane would stay at LouAnn and Billy's. They had three bedrooms, and Paul's had twin beds. Lori Ann was going to sleep in his room, giving up her room for the two of them.

During the day, while Catherine and LouAnn worked, Diane would babysit her niece and nephew until the school year started. Everything sounded good to Catherine except for the excruciating ache in her heart. Would that pain ever go away? Right now, she knew only one thing that would make it better—for Francis to once again tell her she was the only one for him.

The plane suddenly jerked as its wheels touched down and the brakes engaged, landing on ground that she would now call home. She took a deep breath. *Here we go*.

*****

Dressed for work, LouAnn and Mother prepared to leave. Mother dressed in one of the outfits she bought from Eileen. After styling Mom's hair, LouAnn curled and teased her own short black hair, giving it lift on top. She smoothed lipstick over her lips. She was quite stylish and pretty. In fact, both of my sisters, Linda and LouAnn, were pretty, funny, and sweet.

LouAnn showed me the location of everything in the house that I might need while babysitting my nephew and niece, who were eight and three.

The stifling heat of Texas surprised me, but babysitting was actually fun. In the afternoon, we straightened the house before LouAnn and Mother returned.

The weeks rolled by with me spending some weekends at Linda's. She had three children, Normalyn, Kenneth, and

Monica. She and Norm belonged to a motorcycle club. I babysat their kids, too. I was always excited to get to spend time with my sister, Linda. We both enjoyed reading in bed at night.

With August came the beginning of school. The summer hadn't been long enough, but I didn't have any say in the matter. LouAnn took me shopping, and before she finished, she'd bought new color coordinated dresses, shoes, bras, panties, and slips—all for me. Her generosity was overwhelming. Never had I known the joy of owning such pretty things nor started school in such fashion.

*****

Catherine worked directly under LouAnn in the ladies-ready-to-wear department. She learned quickly how to help customers find exactly what they were looking for and in the right size.

Always at the end of her shift, her feet burned from walking for hours. Her back ached from standing, walking, stocking merchantdise, and sizing clothing. Besides the paycheck, the only good thing about working and staying busy was less time for her to think about how much she missed Francis and how her heart would never be the same.

At night, after she laid her head on her pillow, thoughts of where he was right now and what was he doing always flooded her mind. She envisioned him holding Mary, loving her. That was always when she sank into a deep cold, causing her to shiver in the heat of a Texas summer. No matter how many covers she used, she couldn't shake it. Only his arms could remove this cold, and they were in California wrapped around Mary.

More than anything, Catherine wanted her husband back. She wanted them to grow old together, to watch Diane grow up, get married, and have children. She remembered walking down the aisle of that little church in California and the pastor who prayed for her marriage. She wanted to ask God what happened, but she didn't. This might be her punishment.

*****

I caught the bus at seven in the morning. Even though I didn't know anyone yet, I couldn't have been more excited. I wore an orange flowered shift with orange flats to school the first day, and when I needed to change in the locker room for P.E., my slip, bra, and panties all matched!

That afternoon, we had a pep rally. I took a seat in the bleachers, watched the cheerleaders in their cute little skirts, and listened to the students fill the gymnasium with noise. I felt at home until the cheer-leaders hollered, "Come on, ya'll, now yell!" Normal words, really, but their Texas drawl definitely caught me off-guard. *Where in the world am I?* I wondered, thinking I might actually have entered another country!

I could see the football field from the windows of many of my classrooms. In the afternoons, the boys would practice and, I must admit, I enjoyed watching from my desk.

I liked my new school and made some friends. Mary lived across from my sister's house. She had beautiful bleached-blonde hair. Oh, brother, another *Mary*. Anyway, we weren't friends, just acquainttances. Mary's popularity prevented her from hanging out with the new girl at school. Besides, we didn't have any classes together.

The Hurst-Euless-Bedford school district had a similar program to the one in Missouri, but I'd been out of the program for a year now, and the school curriculum in California didn't compare to theirs. This put me considerably behind the other advanced students, so the registrar placed me in honors English and Math classes.

I missed Dad, but I liked it here, or at the very least, I was relieved to be out of L.A. I knew Mother missed him, too. She tried to keep a brave face, but I knew she was heartbroken. I wanted her to be happy.

*****

One September evening, LouAnn cooked spaghetti with salad and garlic bread. Catherine had never cooked spaghetti because Francis didn't like it. It became Diane's favorite dish. Normally, they all sat at the dinner table to eat, but this night, they each took a TV tray and ate in the den while watching a show.

The phone rang and LouAnn went into the kitchen to answer it. "Yes, she's here, just a moment." She took the receiver and pointed it at Catherine. "It's for you. I think it's Francis."

Catherine's pulse quickened and heat filled her cheeks. As she pushed the tray away, her fork fell on the floor, but she hurried to the phone. "Hello."

"Hi, Kid." There was a pause before he continued. "How's it going there?" She could hear a tone in his voice she had heard before, usually when he wasn't sure of himself.

"Oh, fine, fine. I've been working. Diane started school." She tried to keep her voice devoid of emotion. She didn't want him to know how she was dying inside or how good it was to hear him. "How's it going there?" she asked.

"It's not really." His soft voice trailed off.

Her heart skipped a beat. "What? What is it?"

"I had a wreck, totaled the car."
She gasped. "Are you okay?"

He didn't answer right away. "Yeah, I'm okay. You know, I didn't have insurance."

"What are you going to do?" she finally asked.

"Well," he laughed nervously. "I lost my job so I guess I don't need a car."

"Francis, what happened?"

"I miss you and little Gizmo."

She didn't say anything. She would have, but there were no words. Besides, he hadn't said anything about Mary.

"Oh, you know, I'd been drinking. Swerved in front of a truck and got sandwiched between him and a car."

"Did anyone get hurt?"

"No, but I got a DWI. I missed work. They fired me." He sighed. "I guess I'll never work in aerospace again."

Catherine thought a long time before deciding what to say. "Well, you and Mary will figure it out." Why was he calling her? He was supposed to be with Mary.

"There is no Mary and me. We're through."

Catherine stopped breathing, her heart pounding.

"I really miss you," he said again, soft and low.

"I miss you, too."

"I don't know what I'm going to do. I can't pay the rent, so I guess we'll lose everything in the house."

She thought about the couch and chairs, tables, bedroom furniture, and Diane's bike. "You should have a sale and sell it all."

"I'm not as good at that as you are," he said. "I wish you were here. I wish you and Diane were here."

There it was, what he had been dancing around, but not actually saying. She wanted that more than anything, didn't she? Wanted them to all be together again, wanted him to love her again. No, she'd promised Diane they would never go back to Los Angeles.

"We're not coming back. Diane likes her school. Besides, Francis, you don't have a job."

There was an awkward silence and heavy breathing on his end. "Do you think *I* could find work *there*?" he asked.

Catherine closed her eyes, grinning as her heart leapt. "Since when have you not been able to find work? Buck works at Bell Helicopter. Maybe he knows of something."

"Oh, it doesn't matter. I don't have enough money to get there anyway."

"Why don't I come out and help you sell everything? We can fly back together."

"I'd like that, but can you afford it?"

By this time, Diane had finished her dinner and stood next to Catherine. "Is that Daddy?" she asked.

212

"You let me worry about that. Do you want to talk to your daughter? She's right here."

As Catherine handed her daughter the telephone, she felt giddy. He still loved her. He may not even be sure of it yet, but in time, they would be all right. This was the answer to her prayers. She would make arrangements to go as soon as possible and use the money she had been saving for her and Diane a place to live.

*****

The store where Mother worked couldn't keep her job open in her absence. That didn't dissuade her. Nothing could've stopped Mom from going to Dad. I hadn't seen her this happy in a long time. "Your father needs me," she said and then kissed me goodbye.

While Mother was on the west coast, I remained with LouAnn and Billy. Each morning, I rode the bus to school. LouAnn made sure I had a little money not only for lunch, but extra to spend for cokes and candy. I had made a few friends and even had my eye on a particular boy. He played football and we conversed in the mornings before school. George and I shared the same geography class. I tried hard to match his intellect, struggling to raise my hand before his with the correct answers to the teacher's questions. I think we both loved the competition.

Knowing Dad would be returning with Mother and that I didn't have to go back to L.A. was a relief. Mom said he and Mary had split up. That brought a smile to my lips. I wanted him to love Mother again. I wanted her to be happy. I think no child ever wants his or her parents to separate.

LouAnn said she knew how I felt because when she was younger she had wanted Mom to get back together with her dad. Even though that didn't work out, she wanted it to happen for me. Linda, too, voiced her desire for Mom and Dad's reconciliation. We all waited for their return with anticipation.

*****

When Catherine got off the plane at LAX, she expected to hail a taxicab, but upon entering the terminal, she saw Francis waiting at the gate, staring at her. She hesitated only a moment before running into his arms. He held her tightly. Tears of joy moistened her eyes.

"How did you get here? I wasn't expecting to see you." She looked at him and he kissed her, not a long kiss, but one with feeling, creating a heavenly headiness.

"I borrowed a friend's car." His smile made her heart soar.

"I'm glad." She kissed him on the cheek. "You're a sight for sore eyes." She meant that in more ways than one. She saw the red in his eyes, his disheveled hair, and although he had shaved, she saw the tiredness in his frame. Tiredness? Or defeat? Either way, she accepted it. He appeared to welcome her, not only as the one he loved, but as a long lost friend.

He took her home. As they entered the bedroom, their lovemaking was familiar. Months of loneliness melted away. When she awoke with him sleeping beside her, she felt elated. Her bed was no longer empty; the one she loved wanted to start over.

In the light of the morning, after those first two cups of coffee, she rolled up her sleeves and started working. "We need to hang up signs announcing a yard sale this weekend," she told him. "Then we need to price the little things."

"What are we going to do with the little things?"

"After we price them, we'll put them in boxes until this weekend when we'll set it all out on tables." They spent all week going through the things remaining in the house.

Francis cut cardboard and Catherine wrote on it with black crayon. When the weekend arrived, he set up the tables and she arranged all the items. They priced the furniture and brought some of it outside to attract passersby.

Catherine looked and saw Francis pushing Diane's bicycle outside, parking it on the lawn with the other stuff. She took a deep breath. *Well, we can't take it with us,* she thought with a sigh. The night of his car accident, he'd taken his musical instruments along with the sound and recording equipment in the trunk of the car. It had all been destroyed except for his Hagstrom guitar. She planned on him taking that on the plane when they left.

The sale went well and they raised a good sum of money, money that would be desperately needed when they got to Texas. She packed the suitcases with all they decided to salvage.

On Monday, they took a taxi to the airport. Catherine noticed Francis was unusually quiet as he stared out the window.

"I like it here," he finally said. "I wish we could've gotten Gizmo and stayed."

"Francis, I couldn't bring Diane out here. She hated it here."

He nodded. "But Texas? I don't know about that."

She knew he always loved California. If he hadn't been willing to accompany her, then she would have returned alone. She'd promised Diane they would never move back to California.

*****

Catherine's children surprised Francis. Each of them acted as if nothing had happened between him and their mother. Everyone appeared supportive. Buck took Francis to check on a car. It was a

'53 Buick station wagon the owner listed in the paper for sixty dollars.

"How do you like working at Bell Helicopter?" he asked Buck on the way.

"I guess it's a job. It pays the bills."

"Do you know if they're hiring?"

Buck laughed. "Well, I just turned in my notice. So I know they have at least one position for a machinist."

"Oh no, you did?" Francis was disappointed.

"Yeah, we're headed back down to Florida."

"Really?" Francis had hoped to spend some time with Buck. "I thought you'd be here for a while."

"Nah, Virginia doesn't like it here." Buck laughed. "And let's face it, if we stayed here with Larry, Linda, and Norm, I'd be in trouble soon."

Buck didn't need to explain. Francis knew what he meant. LouAnn and Billy would drink a beer, but they didn't go out drinking. Larry, Linda, and Norm were a different story. When Buck drank too much, he usually ended up in a fight—if not with someone else, then with his wife. When some people got drunk, they'd get happy, others cried, but some would fight. Buck was the latter.

"You know, Francis, you and Mom might want to move into our house. The rent we pay is certainly reasonable."

Francis hadn't thought about that. "Maybe." They parked on the street in front of the house with the car in the ad. After looking at the old Buick, Francis thought it might make a good car for the price. He offered fifty dollars, and the owner sold it.

*****

Francis and Catherine rented Buck and Virginia's house. It was located on Bellaire Drive in Hurst, only two miles from Diane's school and close to Bell Helicopter. It was a house they could afford. Most of the homes in the school district were way above their income.

Francis applied at Bell Helicopter and other local companies. He only heard from Murdock Machinery. They offered a wage considerably less than he made at Northrup, but he expected that.

Having secured a car, a job, and a place to live, Francis now had time to reflect on the changes in his life. He still had feelings for Mary. They liked the same things and all had been grand in sunny California. Then the accident happened and he lost his job. Just when they couldn't have been happier, things changed. She had made it clear she never wanted to see him again, but he missed her. What if she had changed her mind? If she wanted to reconcile, she had no way to contact him. Maybe he should call her. No. He had to make this work.

He cared for Catherine, too. She had always been there when he needed her. Besides, he wanted Diane close. The three of them were a family again. He would get over Mary and settle into this new life. Why couldn't he shake these feelings of restlessness? He missed the lights, the freeways, warm breezes and...and Mary.

Francis had promised his folks he would salvage his marriage. At six o'clock sharp Monday morning, he would be at work at Murdock Machinery down Highway 183.

Chapter Seventeen
October 1968

Catherine got a job in the kitchen at Autumn Leaf Nursing Home, but had to work from late in the afternoon until ten at night. Francis worked days, which meant they practically never saw each other. As it turned out, the house was in a different school district. Catherine regretted that Diane had to change schools again and make all new friends.

She knew Francis didn't really like his job, but at least he was trying. He came home every day, and they slept in the same bed at night. He seemed distant, though. Things weren't perfect, but maybe it would only take time. She had been praying that God would show them all the way. She didn't want to live without him and felt blessed to have him back.

Francis bought a used amplifier so he could play his guitar. While she cleaned house on the weekend, he played as he'd always done. She loved his music and understood how much it meant to him. He'd added two new songs to his repertoire and played them often, "The Green, Green Grass of Home" and "Release Me." She struggled when she heard them because the lyrics of the first talked about looking down the road and seeing Mary, but the lyrics of the second haunted her most. The man in the song begged to be released so that he could be with his new love.

Anytime he sat down to play, he always played those two songs. It seemed as if he was trying to tell her something. She began to dread his music. Surely, he knew how much it hurt her. Didn't he care? She thought about talking to him, but what if he only confirmed what she suspected? Their strained relationship stretched to its breaking point, and many times exhaustion overwhelmed her.

*****

Once again, I walked into new classrooms in front of complete strangers who stared as I took the desk the teacher assigned. *I'm not going to like this change at all.* But in my science class, I sat right behind a girl named Janice. We started talking and discovered she lived close to me. Soon, we walked to and from school together.

My new English teacher made literature fun. Our class read *Little Women* and then acted it out. We also read *Romeo and Juliet* and, for extra credit, went to see the movie playing in theaters. Its theme song made it all the way to number one on the music charts. Toward the end of the year, I wrote a commercial—a comedy that involved shaving cream, a pretty model, and a klutzy spokeswoman (me). Everyone laughed, and it was a big hit! My teacher encouraged me to pursue writing.

My American history teacher also employed innovative techniques, making a subject that bores many (not me, but many) exciting and new. One day, we were each giving a presentation when Brad stood and delivered, hands-down, the best one. The class roared, yet its content both informed and entertained. It was absolutely brilliant. I hadn't paid much attention to him before then, but now, I sported a huge crush. He was smart, played football, and was in my English class as well, but, I wasn't the only girl who liked him.

I made another friend, Kim, who invited me over to spend the night. Her family took us out to eat at a Mexican restaurant. I thought to myself, *Oh, boy, I saw this in California—more slop!* I had still never tried it. Her mom insisted, and from the first bite it was true love.

Kim and I went to Six Flags. At first, I didn't think I would get to go, but Mom gave me the money from her paycheck. I had lived in California for almost a year and never went to Disneyland or even Knott's Berry Farm, but Six Flags was great. I loved the rides, especially the thrill ones. Kim's mom dropped us off and we spent the whole day having a blast.

The summer after the eighth grade, Janice, her little brother, Cary, and I walked in the Texas heat to the city pool to go swimming. Janice and I didn't swim, but that wouldn't keep us from flirting with the boys. Besides, maybe Brad would be there.

"You two need to learn to swim," Cary said, while the three of us stood in three feet of water.

"I've always wanted to learn, but I'm scared to death to try," I told him.

He immediately laid face down in the water for several minutes.

"What are you doing?" I screamed when he stood.

"I'm playing dead in the water. You try it," he suggested. "You can always stand up."

I thought about it. *Yes, I could always stand up in three feet of water.*

"Okay, I will."

Right there, I stretched out, face down, and sank, water filling my ears and distorting sounds. I was floating. When I needed air, I simply stood. I laughed at this new discovery. There in the shallow end, I doggy-paddled and eventually kicked my legs and moved my arms, propelling me through the water. Soon, I jumped in from the side and felt exhilarated. Little Cary had taught me how to swim at the age of four-teen. I progressed into deeper water. *Yes! I could swim!*

Mom and Dad appeared to be getting along. They both worked hard. Maybe everything would be okay after all.

*****

August 1969

Every day, Francis went to work at the little machine shop on Highway 183 and then came home. He and Catherine paid the bills and existed together. He spent evenings with Diane while Catherine worked. This had been life for the last eleven months. Still, he couldn't forget California and how free he felt there.

Their little house in Texas suffocated him. Last winter included some freezing cold days and ice. The dreary grayness lasted too long. Then the weather hurled them straight into the heat of the summer.

He could hear the transistor radio Diane and Janice listened to in her room. He didn't like rock 'n roll. That wasn't music. Then the lyrics to a song caught his attention. They were singing about L.A. and being safe and warm. A day of winter with brown leaves and gray skies had those singers California dreamin'. He felt compelled to listen and found himself in the song. He could leave today if he didn't tell her.

It was August now, but soon the leaves would turn brown and the sky gray. He longed for the boulevards of Los Angeles with the sun shining on flowers that always bloomed.

Suddenly, the radio went silent. Diane and her friend bounced out of her room and headed out the back door. He shook his head, trying to clear it.

Why did he no longer have any dreams? It was like he'd failed and there was no hope of change. All the things he believed he could accomplish when he and Catherine married, had all passed. One thing he knew for sure was that he had no future working at that machine shop, but there was nothing else for him to do here. He didn't want to move unless it meant moving back to California. Catherine wouldn't move Diane back there. He felt hopeless.

*****

Catherine grabbed her purse before leaving for work. "Diane, can you do the dishes before bed?" she asked.

"Sure, Mom. I'll see you tonight."

Francis had already started the motor and was waiting. She climbed in and closed the passenger door. She finally broke the silence. "I think we're making roast beef this evening for the residents. You want me to bring some home for you?" Catherine knew Francis liked beef and she didn't have anything else cooked at home.

"No," he answered, but then added, "I guess you can if you want to."

"You and Diane going to grab a hamburger or something?"

"Maybe."

He turned into the circle drive by the door she usually entered. She looked at him and smiled. This was when he kissed her, but today she noticed something distant in his eyes. After that goodbye kiss, he squeezed her arm. "Goodbye, Kid," he said, his eyes gleaming.

"Francis, are you okay?"

He looked straight ahead through the windshield. "Sure. Why do you ask?"

She must be imagining things. "No reason. See you later."

"Okay."

She got out of the car, but before she walked through the door, she looked back and found him staring at her. All that evening, she felt uneasy.

*****

I dried the last plate and put it away as Dad walked through the door. He put his guitar and cord into its case. "I'll be right back," he told me. I watched as he took his guitar and amplifier out to the car.

In a short while, Dad returned. As I was straightening the house, I noticed him in the bedroom packing a suitcase. He went into the bathroom and gathered his toiletries, placing his travel bag in the suitcase. Chills ran down my spine and I had goose bumps.

"What are you doing?" I finally asked.

He stopped, straightened, and looked at me. In his blank face, I recognized sadness. "I can't do this anymore," he said.

What was he talking about? "Do what?"

"Live here."

My pulse quickened. I stared at his open suitcase. "Where are you going?"

"Back to Los Angeles."

"But, Mom..." Surely, he couldn't do this to her again.

He interrupted me. "I don't love your mother anymore. Don't I deserve to be happy?"

I didn't say anything. I wanted both of my parents to be happy.

"Did you tell Mother? Does she know you're leaving?" I asked him, but I already knew the answers.

"No, she'll just make this harder than it has to be."

I watched him close his suitcase. "How are you going to get there?"

"I'm flying out this evening. The airport limo is picking me up at Bellaire and 183." He looked at his watch. "I need to walk down there now or I'll miss it."

I stared as I realized he was actually leaving. It hurt, but somehow, I didn't care. I was numb. He hugged me tightly. "I'll write you and you can come see me," he said.

I followed him out the door. "But Dad, how's Mother going to get home? You should go talk to her." I knew Mother would be devastated. I didn't want him to leave without talking to her.

He started walking down the sidewalk toward 183 with his suitcase in hand. I fell into step beside him.

"There's no time. This is better anyway."

"But what's she going to do when she gets off work tonight?" I pleaded. Mother worked until 10 p.m. We didn't have a phone, so I had no way to contact her and let her know Dad wasn't coming to get her.

"When she realizes I'm not there, she'll probably call LouAnn."

"I don't understand how you can do this. You should have told Mother. She'll wait for no telling how long."

"I can't help that, Diane." Then, as if he were doing a noble thing, he added, "I'm leaving the car."

I walked along the sidewalk with my father. He was leaving and nothing I said would prevent that. We reached the highway, and soon the limo would come. I looked at him with tears in my eyes. "I'll miss you," I cried, but the tears were not for him, they were for Mother, whose heart would break all over again.

He grabbed me, hanging on as if he could take me with him if he never let go.

Then finally, he whispered, "You'd better go on back." As we separated, I saw the tears in his eyes.

"Goodbye," I managed before turning and walking away.

With each step taking me closer to the house, I processed what had happened. Dad wasn't happy here. He was leaving on a jet plane for California. Once again, he had made a choice, one that didn't include Mother or me. I remembered being little and knowing I was Daddy's little girl. He made me feel safe and important to him. I knew I wasn't Daddy's little girl anymore. I didn't make him happy. California, the place that brought me such misery, the place I detested, was the only thing he couldn't live without.

Dad hadn't only rejected Mother, he'd rejected me, too. I finally accepted it. We would no longer play music together or listen to the St. Louis Cardinals' baseball games. From now on, it would just be Mother and me.

When I entered the house, all was quiet. The sun disappeared and darkness fell. Mother would get off work at ten o'clock. I knew she would wait on Dad, thinking he probably stopped for a beer or something. She would call LouAnn only as a last resort and by then, it would probably be eleven or later.

I thought about the distance to where she worked, probably a mile or so. There was a field of darkness between home and there because of no streetlights. The thought of walking through it scared me. *How could I let Mom know not to wait?*

I finally decided to walk. I'd take Oscar with me. He was a big dog and would provide protection if anyone bothered me. We started out in the dark early enough to be there before Mother got off work and stood outside. Oscar didn't need a leash. He walked along beside me. Walking north toward Pipeline Road, we soon left the houses and passed the elementary school. Entering the field, darkness surrounded me. Crickets chirped, an owl screeched, and I jumped, but Oscar remained at my side. It was a quarter of a mile at least before the field emptied into a shopping center with lights in the parking lot. From there, I could cross Pipeline and walk a little further before reaching Autumn Leaf Lodge.

*****

Catherine punched the time clock, grabbed her purse, and walked outside. She expected to see the Buick and Francis waiting in the circle. Instead, she recognized the wag of a familiar tail and saw Diane sitting on the bench in front.

"Diane, Honey, what are you doing here?" she asked, looking for any sign of the car.

Her daughter took a deep breath. "It's just me, Mom. Dad's not coming."

Catherine didn't know why, but all day she'd had this sinking feeling. There was something in the way Francis acted when he dropped her off.

As they began walking home together, Diane told her about the evening and what Francis had said. Why didn't he say something to her? She was confused and angry. Pain stabbed her chest and a lump rose in her throat.

"So, he's gone back to L.A. Of course, he didn't want to talk to me! He's a coward!" Once again, he'd left her. Once again, she was alone. Well, she had Diane. They had each other.

"You said he packed up his guitar?" Catherine asked her.

"Yes. The amp, too."

"But he didn't take them with him to the airport?"

"No. He took them to the car and left, but then he came back in a little bit."

"Did he say anything about Mary?"

"No. He asked, 'Didn't he deserve to be happy?'"

Happy? Catherine realized he'd never cared whether she or Diane was happy. She wondered what happiness really was.

She considered the courage it took for her daughter to come meet her. Catherine placed her arm around Diane. "I'm sorry, Honey, that you had to walk all this way in the dark."

As Diane told her about the walk and how Oscar protected her, Catherine thought, *What kind of man could be so self-absorbed to not even consider the safety of his child above his own happiness?* He should have known Diane would try to meet her. He could have had the common decency to tell her himself that he was leaving, maybe even deliver the car to the lodge in the daylight and walk back home.

Chapter Eighteen

Catherine parked the Buick in front of Jackson's Pawn Shop on Pipeline Rd. She grabbed her purse and the pawn ticket she'd found on the table beside her bed. When she walked through the door, a man in a t-shirt and overalls met her.

"Can I help you, Ma'am?" He had a mustache and a cigar in his mouth.

She handed him the ticket. "I'd like to get this guitar out."

He took the ticket and went behind the counter. Thumbing through a box, he pulled out another. "Okay, you want the amplifier, too?"

"Yes, everything that was pawned," she answered and opened her wallet.

He left and went into the back room. In a few minutes, he returned with the guitar case and amplifier. When she realized Francis most likely pawned the guitar to purchase his airfare, she resolved to retrieve the instrument and decided Diane should have it.

Once back home, despair overwhelmed her. She and Diane were alone again. Francis was gone, but the rent, utilities, and bills were not. She stared out the front window, feeling lost. Morning turned into afternoon. At the sight of LouAnn's black Ford pulling into the driveway, Catherine drew a deep breath, lifted her chin, and opened the door.

She couldn't hide her bitterness when she told LouAnn about the pawnshop. "He must have pawned the guitar to buy the airline ticket. I had to get it out," she explained. "I had to get it out for Diane."

"But not so he can have it back, right?" LouAnn asked.

"No, that guitar's for Diane."

"When's the last time she played, Mom?"

Catherine hesitated. "She's had other things on her mind, that's all. Besides, if she never plays again, that guitar is Diane's."

LouAnn nodded. They sat across from each other at the table, each with a cup of coffee. "So, Mom, can you afford to still live here?"

The question didn't surprise Catherine. When she did the math, her heart sank. She only earned minimum wage, $1.65 an hour, with a schedule of twenty-five to thirty hours a week. "The rent is 125 a month. That's not utilities or anything else. I'm just not sure." She hoped LouAnn had some suggestions.

"Well, the problem is, Mom, I don't know where else you could move around here where the rent would be less."

Catherine understood that as well. She needed to live close to her job and didn't want Diane to have to change schools yet again. "I'll have to stay here until I can find someplace."

"But, Mom, how will you and Diane eat?"

"We'll manage somehow."

"Well, I have an idea." LouAnn's voice sounded hopeful. "I've talked to Mr. Schwartz and he's agreed to hire you back, same wage but thirty-six to thirty-eight hours a week."

Catherine sighed with relief. "Oh, that would help. Bless Mr. Schwartz's heart."

"Great. So I can tell him you'll resign and be to work in two weeks?"

Catherine smiled and nodded. "The sooner the better."

The front door opened and Diane called out, "I'm home, Mom." Catherine looked at the clock on the wall. It was almost four o'clock.

"We're in here, Honey. Come join us."

"Hi, LouAnn." Diane grabbed a cookie from the jar.

"Diane, Mom and I have been talking about money." LouAnn glanced at Catherine briefly.

Diane stopped chewing. "It's not good, is it?"

"We'll be fine," Catherine said.

LouAnn spoke up. "I've talked to Mr. Schwartz. I told him how smart you are. I even mentioned your honors classes. He's willing to offer you a job, but you have to work at his second store."

"What? Are you serious?" Diane's excitement was evident. Until now, she had only babysat.

"LouAnn," Catherine scolded.

"But, I'm fourteen. Isn't that too young to work?"

"I told him you're going on sixteen. Once you have your birthday in a couple of weeks, then you *will* be going on sixteen." LouAnn's eyes gleamed. "He's agreed to pay you under the table until you're legal."

"LouAnn!" Catherine's stern voice startled even her, but she needed to put a stop to this right now. "Diane needs to focus on school. She has a new science honors class as well as honors English and math. I don't want her to sacrifice her education."

"No, Mom. I can handle it. I want to work. And the other store is perfect. It's not far from school."

Catherine shook her head. "I don't know," she hesitated.

"Mom, Diane's a teenager. If she has a job, at least she can help pay for those things she'll need."

As Diane continued to beg, Catherine considered her youngest daughter.

Maybe she *could* handle school and work at this early age. LouAnn was probably right. At least this way Diane wouldn't have to do without things Catherine couldn't provide. Perhaps it did make sense.

*****

When the bell rang at the end of the school day, I rushed to gather my books and walk to work at the store on Highway 183. Along my way, I passed a drive-in where they made a grilled ham and cheese sandwich that was to-die-for. I ordered one and took it to work for my dinner break that evening. My shift ended at nine. Mom, who got off work at the same time, usually picked me up about fifteen minutes later.

I felt so grown up having a job. My friends envied me. Usually, when I got off work, Mom and I would talk, but then I needed to do my homework. The first class in which I found myself struggling was English. This semester focused on writing, but the homework was brutal. I also had joined the creative writing club.

My teacher asked me to stay after class one day. She told me she was confused about my performance. I didn't want to, but found myself pouring out my story to her— you know, the pitiful girl whose father left and she had to go to work to help support the family. I played it up for all it was worth! I had never been in this situation before, having to give an excuse for not doing well. Afterward, I felt awful.

A few days later, the school counselor summoned me. I had no idea why. She asked a series of questions about my home life. Was my father living at home? She asked if I liked my job. She asked a sort-of "what do you want to be when you grow up" question.

Then, her head aligned with mine and she looked directly into my eyes. "Do you feel like your circumstances will prevent you from accomplishing what you want to do with your life?"

I knew what she was asking. She wanted to know if I had lost hope. Of all the things I had lost, hope was not one of them. I had learned to pray for what I needed. I prayed for Mom. I prayed that my dad would turn to Jesus. I even prayed that God would send the right man to share life with me.

I thought carefully about how to answer. "No," I replied confidently. "I feel like I'll be able to do whatever I want. If I want to be a doctor or a lawyer, I can do it."

She seemed satisfied with this answer. As I left her office, I figured it was probably good I didn't share with her what I really wanted to be. I smiled, walking down the hallway back to class. My desire: fall in love, get married, and raise a family—that was all. But if God had something else in mind, so be it.

*****

On Saturday, while Catherine washed laundry, the doorbell rang. A man in a suit stood on the doorstep.

"Are you Mrs. Burch?" He carried a file of papers.

"Yes. Who's asking?"

He was a bill collector for a company from which Francis had taken out a loan. She was familiar with the debt. This was the only address on file, and since she didn't have a telephone, he came to collect in person. It didn't matter that she and Francis weren't living together, her responsibility remained the same.

"I can't pay that right now," she told him. "But, hopefully, I can make that payment by the first," she lied.

He told her if she didn't, they'd file a claim in court.

When she closed the door and turned around, Diane stood in the hallway. "Who was that?"

"He was a bill collector." Catherine no longer tried to shield Diane from their troubles. Instead, she welcomed her teenager's support. She shook her head. "I don't know what we're going to do. I think we need to move to that garage apartment on Bedford-Euless Road."

Catherine had been searching for a cheaper house to rent. She had only found a garage apartment located a block from her work. She hadn't rented it because it was attached to a vacant and rundown house. The garage apartment had been a more recent remodel, but the small dwelling consisted of one room for the living area and bedroom, with the kitchen separated only by a bar. The bathroom was a small room off the kitchen. The upside—she could reduce their rent by half, and Diane wouldn't have to change schools.

"It's okay. If we have to, we have to." Diane hugged her. "It'll all work out."

Catherine threw her hands up in the air. "I hope your dad's happy! We all know *he* deserves to be happy!" Catherine didn't refrain from sharing her emotions with her daughter. She blamed him for every hardship they both endured.

*****

1969

In late fall, Catherine moved herself and Diane into the little garage apartment on Bedford-Euless Road. Catherine provided as best she could, but often wondered if Diane felt poor or embarrassed about where she lived. Most of her daughter's classmates lived in nice homes and didn't have to work after school.

When Diane started dating, Catherine knew she'd need clothes and makeup.

Working for a clothing store meant discounts. If she couldn't give her daughter other things, at least she could buy her nice clothes. As soon as she learned prices were to be reduced, she caught great styles for less.

Soon, Catherine had Southwestern Bell install a telephone. Francis had written and even called a couple of times on Diane's birthday and at the holidays. He told their daughter he worked as a used car salesman at a lot in Long Beach. He didn't make much money, but he sent her a typewriter for Christmas.

Once, when Francis called, Catherine insisted on talking with him. The conversation started out strained, but when she kept it at only small talk, he seemed to relax. She asked him for the number of the lot where he worked in case of an emergency. When Catherine hung up, she wondered why things had to be this way. She missed him more than ever.

She and Diane lived in the garage apartment for a year before the land sold out from under them. Once again, Catherine needed to find someplace to live. What if she couldn't find anywhere else? All appeared hopeless when a young man, who Diane was dating at the time, had a paper route in the area. He told her about an apartment complex across the highway from Bell Helicopter. He said the rent for a one bedroom was a hundred and five dollars, utilities included. They could afford that!

Catherine met with the apartment manager and signed a lease on a one bedroom that had central air and heat. Diane's eyes got big as saucers upon seeing the swimming pool in front of their door. The apartment even had a dishwasher. Maybe Francis had walked away from providing for them, but God hadn't. He proved His provision all the time. Still, Catherine couldn't help but worry.

The old Buick limped on its last leg. If it quit on them, she didn't know what she'd do. One day, the phone rang.

"Hi, Mommy." It was Buck who worked at a car dealership in Florida. "I have great news! The lot here is repossessing a '63 Mercury not far from you and you can have it."

"What do you mean?"

"My boss said all we have to do is get someone to go get it, and it's yours!"

"Really? Who's going to go get it?"

"Don't worry about that. I'll take care of everything."

After hanging up, she marveled at this good fortune.

When nighttime arrived, Catherine's bed was no long empty because she shared a bed with Diane. Still, loneliness over-whelmed her. It might not be the right thing, but she hoped Francis was lonely, too.

Life hadn't turned out like she'd hoped. The difficult days left her bitter and complaining about everything.

*****

1971

A trunk line light on the switchboard flashed and buzzing ensued. I plugged the metal end of the left cord into the hole.

"L.D. Bell High School. How may I help you?" I spoke strong and sure, proud of my job.

"I need to speak to the registrar's office, please."

"Yes, I'd be happy to connect you. Who may I say is calling?" After the lady on the phone told me her name, I plugged the metal end of the right cord into the corresponding hole for Mrs. Buzby, the school registrar. I announced the caller, transferred the call, and then returned to the office typing.

My dad had sent a typewriter the previous Christmas. Linda showed me the home keys and told me to practice. Thus, I had a head start in typing class. This skill proved valuable for any office setting.

At the end of my sophomore year, I had applied for a job in the school office. The high school hired me for a position that paid twenty cents more than minimum wage and offered a forty-hour work week during the summer. I worked all summer until the first of August, making more money than I had ever made. Then, when school started again, I worked before and after school and one period during the day, giving me my evenings free.

Over the Thanksgiving holiday, my friend, Susan, and I hung out, driving around in Mom's car and listening to the hits on the radio. While we were driving, we noticed a beautiful metallic blue car with racing stripes and a solid red license plate. We must have seen it at least a dozen times. Sunday afternoon, Susan and I were sitting in the apartment complex parking lot, talking and listening to the radio, when suddenly, that same car whizzed by behind us. There was no reason for this car to be here unless it was following us.

We looked at each other. I started the car, backed out, and sped off in pursuit. The car turned on Pipeline Road and I pushed down on the accelerator, trying to catch it. Zooming down the four-lane road, I traveled at seventy miles per hour in a thirty-five. Whoever was in the car definitely didn't want us to catch him, but I was on a mission.

Just before reaching Loop 820, the blue car pulled into the McDonald's on the left. I followed. A soldier in fatigues jumped out of the hot rod. After introductions, I learned his name was Rick and he lived in the same apartments, thus giving him reason to be there. I felt foolish! Though he offered to buy us a hamburger, we declined and returned home.

Later that afternoon, while Susan and I were talking in the car, Rick walked over and joined us. He had just returned from the war and was stationed at Bell Helicopter. I felt flattered he paid any attention to us at all.

With Bell Helicopter right across the street from our apartment, Mom and I had become accustomed to the sound of choppers flying overhead. The Vietnam War raged on, and helicopters played a major role.

I was seventeen and Rick was more than four years older. During the first week after we met, he kept his distance and didn't even try to hold my hand. He apparently only wanted to be friends. We saw each other every day. In the evenings, he serenaded me with his guitar and kept me laughing. Not that his serenading made me laugh, just that he could add humor to any circumstance.

"So, why were you so late getting home today?" he asked one evening.

"I had to walk to my Mom's store. We only have one car. Mom usually drops me off at school because she needs the car. After school, I walk to get it."

He reached in his pocket, pulled out his keys, and threw them to me. "Why don't you drive my car to school?"

I threw them back. "Ha, ha! Very funny!" I said.

Rick's metallic blue '71 Duster had four-on-the-floor, a Holly 750 double pumper carburetor, and racing stripes. I didn't for one minute think he meant it.

"No, I'm serious. I don't need it. I can walk to work. It's just across the street."

Overcome with excitement, I jumped up, snatched the keys from his hand, and said, "Why don't I just drive it now?"

The next night while he and I went driving around, listening to the radio, I exclaimed, "You should've been with me today. Oh, wow! It was great!" I couldn't contain my enthusiasm. "I pulled into the school parking lot and everyone turned to see who was driving the hot rod! After school, I outran this senior in a Camaro."

"A Camaro? That's not even a challenge!" He beamed.

Melanie finished singing the lyrics, "I've got a brand new pair of roller skates, you've got a brand new key" on the radio. The weather forecast was next. "Those temperatures are going to get low tonight, folks. It's going to dip down into the lower twenties. It's time to get that antifreeze in the car, if you haven't gotten around to it by now."

I looked at Rick. "The lower twenties! Mom's at work and she hasn't put antifreeze in the car yet."

"Why don't we go get her car and I'll get it ready before it freezes outside," he offered.

"Oh, that's great. You don't mind?"

"No, I'd like to help."

Our eyes met and I smiled.

Two hours later, Rick and I returned Mom's car ready for the freeze tonight. Then we both got back in his car and headed home. The loud and clear radio broadcast ran through its station identification.

"You're listening to WGN, Chicago!"

I looked at Rick. "What are you doing listening to Chicago?"

He chuckled. "I don't know what the local stations are. I just listen to what comes in clear."

"Well, no wonder it's going to get down below freezing. It's Chicago!"

He shook his head. "Your mother's going to think I'm crazy!" We laughed together.

"How in the world are you picking up a station from Chicago all the way in Texas?" We marveled at how strong its signal must have been.

"Well, at least your mom already has antifreeze in her car."

I glanced at him seriously. "Thanks, that was really nice, by the way."

Chapter Nineteen

Darkness claimed the evening as I freshened my makeup and curled my eyelashes. I heard the knock on the door. He was here. Quickly, I stashed everything in the bathroom drawer and went to answer it.

I pushed back the curtains and opened the sliding glass door. The reflection of the inside lights flickered in Rick's brown eyes. "You're here. Come on in," I told him. Beneath his leather jacket, he wore a white turtleneck, which accentuated his tanned face and black hair. I looked away, carefully concealing my attraction to him. After all, he apparently only wanted to be friends and I just loved being with him.

He came in and closed the door. "I'm not too early, am I?"

"No, huh-uh." I walked away. "There's a couple of things I have to do first. I should only be a minute." I straightened the bathroom and then wiped off the kitchen counter. "I want everything to be clean when Mom gets home from work," I explained. I thought I saw his eyes change when I said that.

"So we're going downtown Fort Worth?" he asked.

Since moving here about eight weeks ago, Rick hadn't learned his way around. I had promised to take him to Leonard's downtown to do some Christmas shopping.

"Yeah, but first I have a homework assignment I have to finish. Is that okay?"

I plopped on the sofa, opened my book, and unfolded the sheet of paper.

He sat not far from me. "Can I help?"

"No, it'll just take me a minute." I wrote down the answer to the first question and turned the page, looking for the answer to the next. He moved closer with what I thought was curiosity. His hand touched my neck, rubbing gently. Then he brushed my blonde hair away from my face. The room grew hotter. I could no longer read the questions so I slammed the book closed and looked at my watch.

"Wow, I guess we'd better go. I can finish this later." I grabbed my purse and we walked out together. When we got in the car, he sat in the driver's seat and didn't move.

"What's wrong?" I questioned.

He laughed. "You got my keys?"

"Oh, yeah!" I scrambled to find the keys in my purse.

We drove and talked and laughed. Spending time with Rick made the world seem brighter. It took me a few minutes to process his actions on the sofa, but when I did, my heart leapt with joy. *He wanted to be more than friends!*

When we returned, he parked the car and shut off the engine, but we continued talking and laughing. His eyes stared into mine. There, in the moonlight, I couldn't breathe as he leaned close. His lips tenderly, almost timidly, caressed mine, as if he was searching for my feelings. The earth moved, my heart soared, and I got lost in his embrace. His lips claimed mine as his arms pulled me closer. He was every bit a gentleman and respected my innocence. Even though I had dated, intimacy I saved for the one I married.

One of the first places we went together was church. We planned to marry that summer, but by March, we could wait no longer. Mother approved of him, which helped in many ways. I didn't care if Dad approved or not. Mom and I didn't have money for a wedding, so I was content with going to a Justice of the Peace.

Larry and his wife, Susan, stood up with us and we were married on March 31, 1972. Linda and LouAnn made a wedding cake and prepared a small family reception at Larry's house. I couldn't have been happier. At the age of seventeen, God had answered my prayer and sent the right man into my life.

Rick and I moved into a brand new upscale apartment in Euless. He owed the

Army another year, but wouldn't reenlist because the Army might send him somewhere I couldn't go.

*****

After a long day at work, Catherine finally climbed between the sheets and felt the ache of every muscle and joint in her body. That didn't bother her nearly as much as the emptiness beside her and the deafening silence. She missed Diane lying next to her and their light conversations before going to sleep.

She had always known one day Diane would leave the nest and she would be alone. She wanted her youngest child to be happy. Now that she was gone, Catherine would have to get used to it.

After all this time, she still clung to a hope that Francis would one day return, one day remember telling her "she was the one he wanted" and his promise to "push her wheelchair when she grew old." Old? Was she there? It was hard to believe she would turn sixty later this year.

Catherine thought about her life. She remembered the early years with Kenneth on the farm. She thought about Essie and their parents. Her mom and dad had been in heaven a long time now. Precious memories flooded her mind and tears rolled down the sides of her face. She remembered meeting Francis. She closed her eyes and let herself relive those days, recalling the "Tennessee

Waltz." She remembered their picnic in the autumn air, his tenderness, her heart as it thrilled at his attention. Her eyelids grew heavy and she fell asleep, dreaming.

Smoke filled the apartment making it difficult to see. Catherine panicked as she suddenly realized Diane wasn't there. Something was wrong. Diane should be here. Quickly, she moved through the small apartment, searching and calling for her youngest daughter. Her heart pounded. She must find her before it was too late. She couldn't find Diane anywhere in the apartment. She pushed back the sliding glass door and stepped outside in the darkness. The moon shone down on the sidewalk. The pool light illuminated the water. Slowly, she put one foot in front of the other, dreading each step. Like a magnet, the water drew Catherine closer to its edge. She trembled with fear. As she approached, she could see hair, blonde hair, fanned out in the water. She looked closer at the body floating face down and recognized the jeans and pink shirt. "Oh, no! No, no, no!" she screamed and sat up straight in the bed.

The room was quiet and dark. It was a nightmare. A terrible nightmare. *Only a dream, thank God.* Catherine thought she understood what the dream meant. In a way, Diane had left, certainly not drowned, but she had lost her little girl. In only a month, Rick would be getting out of the army and the two of them would move to San Francisco for three months before returning to Amarillo and Rick's new job.

*****

1973

I woke up in time to see the "Welcome to California" sign on the side of the road as our car passed by. I never thought I'd return to California, but with Rick by my side, I had changed my mind. He had three months of training to complete in San Francisco.

We had driven all the way from Fort Worth, pulling a U-Haul trailer behind our car—our next stop, Long Beach. Rick hadn't met my dad and it only made sense to stop in and see him on our way up the coast.

Dad was glad to see us and thrilled to know we'd be in San Francisco for a short period. By this time, things had changed considerably for him. Dad now owned a used car lot. He introduced me to his girlfriend, Ginny, who was about his age, and the four of us went out to eat. It hurt seeing him with someone else, but I tried to be friendly. Mother loved Dad. I knew she wanted him to return to her someday. Now, observing him with Ginny, that hope slipped farther away.

After Rick and I got settled in San Francisco, I decided to try to reconnect with Dad. I flew to visit him for a few days.

Then, he and Ginny were going to drive me back to San Francisco.

Dad lived in a luxury apartment in a much nicer area than Lawndale, where he, Mother, and I had lived. Ginny baked a ham for dinner. Since he only had one bedroom, I slept on the sofa. I felt like a stranger in my dad's new life and had difficulty falling asleep. Hearing a noise, I realized someone was walking about. I opened my eyes to see Ginny, stark naked, walking through the living room to the kitchen where she got a drink. I quickly closed my eyes and feigned sleep.

The next day over coffee, Dad told me he was going to divorce Mom. He wanted to marry Ginny. Shocked and concerned for Mother, I asked, "Does Mom know?"

"No. She doesn't have to know. I can place an ad in the newspaper for a period of time and when she doesn't respond, I can have a divorce." He sort of shrugged his shoulders.

How easy it appeared for him to rid himself of past obligations. Dad drove a nice car, took me to a fancy restaurant, and flashed a green stack of bills in his wallet. I wanted to feel happy for him, I really did, but I couldn't stop thinking about Mom and her struggles, all the times she'd done without just so she could provide for me.

The next day, Dad let me drive one of the cars from his lot so I could visit a friend in Lawndale. I enjoyed driving on the freeway and seeing my old friend, Teresa. Afterward, though, I couldn't stop thinking about what he'd said. He was going to divorce Mother and she wouldn't even know it. My stomach churned. How could Dad do that? She deserved better. Outraged, I stopped the car at a pay phone and placed a collect call to Mom.

I broke the news. "Mom, Dad has a girlfriend." There was silence while I waited for a response.

"Oh?"

"Yes, and he told me he was going to divorce you."

"He can't. I won't let him."

"He says he can put it in the paper and after a certain amount of time, if you don't respond, he can have a divorce."

"That's if he doesn't know where I am, and we both know he does." I was glad to hear the determination in Mother's voice.

"Mom, I want you to fight it." I was becoming angrier and angrier. "I'll testify for you. He should have to pay some kind of back child support or alimony or something."

"Well, I'll think about it. You call me when you get back home."

*****

The following week, Catherine experienced restless nights and a pain in the pit of her stomach. Each day, it became more and more difficult to prepare for work. She couldn't stop thinking about what Diane had told her. Francis's intention to obtain a divorce hadn't impacted her nearly as much as what Diane had said before. "*Mom, Dad's got a girlfriend.*"

That single statement dashed all the hopes to which Catherine had clung. He wasn't coming back. The promises he made all those years ago meant nothing. She wasn't the one he wanted. The room started spinning and she felt faint. Every action, every movement took all her strength.

She got out of bed and started getting dressed for work when another sharp pain stabbed in her stomach. The pain increased and she tried everything to relieve it as she continued to dress for her daily shift at the department store. When she arrived at work, her coworkers realized something was wrong. They gave her a Coca Cola, suggesting it might be gas in her stomach causing the pain, but the Coke only made it worse.

She left the store to return home, and by the time she arrived, all she could do was collapse on the bed. She managed to pick up the phone and call Linda.

"Linda," she said breathlessly. "Please call an ambulance. I can't move."

*****

The sun hadn't completely risen when someone started pounding on the glass of our bedroom window. Rick quickly jumped up and went to the front door.

Our apartment manager stood outside. "I have an emergency phone call for your wife. Tell her to hurry, they're holding."

I stepped into my slippers and grabbed my robe. Hurrying out the door, I tied the belt as I ran. Rick and I had decided to save the cost of having a telephone installed in our San Francisco apartment since we'd be leaving soon for Amarillo. I had given the apartment manager's number to anyone who might need to contact us.

My adrenaline rushed, my mind raced, and my hands shook. Who could be calling and why? Something awful must have happened. I walked in his door and he handed me the phone receiver that had been lying on the desk.

"Hello," I said.

"Oh, Diane, Honey, it's Linda. I'm afraid...I have some bad news."

I could literally hear my heart pounding in my ears. "What? What is it?"

"Mom's in the hospital in ICU. They did exploratory surgery. The doctor said she had an ulcer that perforated right where the stomach empties into the bowel."

"Well, how is she?"

Linda paused a moment. "The doctor said the next twenty-four hours will tell. I think he's concerned she might have an infection in her bloodstream. Something about them trying to get everything that spilled into her abdomen."

"Are you saying she might die?"

I heard Linda exhale. "They just don't know, Honey."

"Well, I'll get on a plane and be there as fast as I can. I'll call you back in an hour or so with my flight info."

"Okay, Honey. I'll meet you at the airport."

As we said our goodbyes, I thought about my options. Rick and I didn't have much money. He took a sizeable cut in pay when he left the Army for his civilian job. I wasn't working right now, and the move here had taken most of our resources. I had to get to Texas fast. Mother needed me.

After I dropped Rick off at work, I drove to the nearest pay phone. I heard Dad answer and then the operator spoke as I had instructed her. "I have a collect call from Diane Yates. Will you accept the charges?"

"Yes, I will."

I quickly told Dad what Linda had said.

"Well, that doesn't sound good," he agreed. "What are you going to do?"

"I want to go be with her, but I don't have the money. I was wondering if I could borrow it from you."

"I'll call the airline and get it taken care of," he told me.

"Thanks, Dad." And then, "I love you."

"I love you, too." He never failed to tell me that, but right now it sounded better somehow. He'd invested little in my teenage years. Somehow, I equated him buying my ticket now with love. I didn't know when I'd have the money to repay Dad, but then I thought if I didn't ever repay him, it was the least he could do.

Then he said, "Let me know how she's doing." This request was the first sign he might have any concern for Mother.

"I will."

Two hours later, Rick kissed me goodbye at the airport and I boarded a 727 for Dallas. When I arrived, Linda was waiting for me at the gate. She filled me in on the latest as we quickly drove from Dallas to the hospital.

Fort Worth had three very good hospitals capable of handling any situation, but Mother didn't have money or insurance, so she had to be admitted to the less-desirable county hospital.

When I entered her room, I wasn't prepared for what I saw. My jaw dropped and tears stung my eyes. A tube ran up her nose, down her throat, and into her stomach, pumping out dark fluid. The IV in her arm had bruising around it.

LouAnn hugged me and explained. "She sleeps from all the pain medicine. They made a large incision the full length of her stomach because they didn't know what was wrong."

"Is she…is she going to be all right?"

LouAnn shook her head. "The doctor said if she makes it twenty-four hours and has no infection, she should be fine."

I nodded and thought I knew how to pray. I held Mom's hand as she slept. Linda, LouAnn, and I all waited and comforted one another.

When Mother awoke, she saw me beside her. "Hi, Mom." I patted her hand. "Everything's going to be all right. You rest and we'll talk later." Her eyes closed and she slept again.

In the morning, the doctor told us the blood showed no infection. "I think she should be fine," he said. "We'll keep her in the hospital about a week. She'll need to take it easy for a while. In about six weeks or so, she can probably return to work."

Seriously? Mother couldn't work for six weeks! Mom couldn't afford not working. I worried for her. Then I got an idea.

The next day, I walked into the department store where Mother worked. Everyone wanted to know how she was doing and were glad to hear she would be okay.

I found the owner of the store and asked to talk to him. "Mr. Schwartz, I was wondering if you would consider letting me work in Mother's place while she's in the hospital."

He nodded thoughtfully. "Yes, I think that would be fine."

I breathed a sigh of relief. He liked my idea. "I could clock in on her time card and my time could be on her paycheck."

He placed his hand on my shoulder. "You come in and work anytime. Leave whenever you need to."

Since Mother and I came to Texas five years ago, this man had been a godsend in many ways.

One of the sales ladies got my attention. "Diane." She was carrying a tree with leaves made of bills of various denominations. "We have a money tree for your Mom. We'd like for you to take it to her."

"Of course." I looked into the caring eyes of all the staff gathered around me. "Thank you guys so much."

Mom steadily improved. They removed the tube. All the cards and the thoughtfulness of the money tree touched

Humans writing

her. After twelve days in the hospital, the doctor finally released her to go home. I stayed for two weeks before returning to California. I intended to stay longer, but missed Rick immensely.

Even though LouAnn lived in Millsap, a little over an hour away, Linda lived close by. Mother relied on her in our absence. I was thankful Linda had been there for Mom.

Chapter Twenty
Fall 1973

Catherine punched the time clock on the back wall of the stockroom. It had been three months since her surgery. She'd been back at work now almost six weeks. She'd been told she barely escaped death.

Catherine didn't even know she had an ulcer. The excruciating pain began when it perforated, tearing the bowel. The distress she experienced from learning about Francis's new love sent her over the edge.

As long as she didn't know about Francis, she could hang onto the hope he'd return. How was she going to live without him? Up until now, she had lived one day at a time, but always with hope that tomorrow might be different. All her dreams she held dear, all that mattered, had slipped through her fingers. Did she dare continue to hope?

"Mrs. Burch," Mr. Schwartz caught her just before she left the stockroom. "What do you hear from those kids?" By "those kids" she knew he meant Diane. She stood straight and forced a smile, dragging herself out of her thoughts.

"Well, they're in Amarillo now. And the latest news—they're expecting."

"Oh, really? I bet you're excited."

"I am. And you know what this means—you need to let me know when the baby clothes are going on sale so I can start buying things."

He chuckled. "Will do, will do. Now, how far is Amarillo from here?"

"I think it's about three hundred miles. LouAnn, Linda, and I are going to visit in a few weeks."

At the mention of LouAnn's name, they talked a few minutes more. LouAnn had been Mr. Schwartz's favorite employee, but then she moved to Millsap. He often asked about her. She had been the reason Catherine and Diane worked there in the first place.

After Catherine's shift, she shopped in the baby department, buying a baby blanket and some onesies. At home, there was a box in the closet where she had begun storing clothes and necessities for the baby.

Catherine had sixteen grandchildren, including four stepchildren. With her always having children at home, she had never really been in a position to enjoy her grandchildren like most grandmothers. Now that her youngest was grown, she wanted things to somehow be different with Diane's children.

That night, she stared at the ceiling through the darkness and thought about Francis, much like every night. She couldn't let go. She'd envisioned a time when Diane would give birth to their first grandchild—hers and Francis's. She'd always thought he would be right there, holding her hand, and sharing in her joy. That didn't seem to matter to him now. She didn't matter to him.

Hearing about her daughter's doctor visits excited her but made her wish she could be there during the pregnancy. How she missed her youngest. Diane told her about the church they attended and all the friends they'd made. She and Rick seemed truly happy, but why did they have to live so far away?

*****

1976

Doris, my boss, placed the call on hold. "Diane, it's your husband on line one."

I quickly picked up the phone. "Hi, is everything okay?"

"You're not going to believe this, but the movers called and they can move us today if we want them to."

"What? I didn't think they were supposed to come until next week."

"I know, but they're in the area and wanted to know if it was okay. I told them I'd check with you."

"I'm not ready for them to move us today."

"But, they'll do it all anyway," he reasoned.

That morning I had left for my last day at work, expecting to have the next week to prepare for the move. "Why not? Tell them to go ahead." Rick and I were nothing if not spontaneous!

We had lived in Amarillo for almost three years now. I was sad to leave our church and our many friends, but I was happy to return to Fort Worth. I yearned to live close to Mother and my sisters.

By the time I got off work, the movers had emptied our house. Rick loaded our suitcases and little Brian in the station wagon, and we pointed the car toward home. Our son, Brian, would turn two this May. Mother was crazy about him. She came and stayed with me before his birth and three weeks after.

Five months later, Brian started crawling. Dad and Ginny came to visit then. Ginny and I had little in common, making our time together tense. I had prayed for Dad since I was eleven because I knew he had never asked God to forgive him. I'm not sure Dad had ever asked anyone to forgive him, least of all God. I prayed but lacked the courage to talk with him. What a difference God could make in Dad's life. I began praying for Ginny, too.

Once in Fort Worth, Rick and I bought a three-bedroom brick home in Richland Hills, not far from Mom. Two springs later, our baby girl, Christa, entered into this world. Brian expressed his disap-pointment at having a sister instead of a brother by beating a plant in the living room with his Hot Wheels track. But when he held her in his arms and let her little fingers wrap around his, he decided she would do.

Rick and I had our two children and jobs we loved. All was perfect in our eyes, but God had other plans. When Christa was only nine months old, I discovered I was pregnant again—much to my horror. I didn't want another child, especially not now. This meant two in diapers at the same time, more laundry, and no sleep. I went to the doctor appointments begrudgingly. I took vitamins and got fat begrudgingly. For six months my pregnancy progressed despite my reluctance with no excitement from me. I had three months left before the delivery date, when I went to a regularly scheduled appointment.

The doctor listened to my tummy with his stethoscope. "So how are you feeling?"

"Well, I've been having some cramping, but I'm better now."

He frowned. "Why don't you get undressed and let me examine you."

A few minutes later, with my feet in the stirrups, I heard him exclaim. "Whoa!"

"What? What is it?" My heart rate increased.

"You've had some kind of premature labor." He removed his gloves and tossed them in the trashcan. "You're completely effaced and dilated to four."

I shook my head. "What are you saying?" I worked at a hospital and for a neonatologist so I already knew what he was saying.

"I need you on complete bed rest now," he confirmed, "or this baby may be in your neonatal unit. I don't need to tell you what chances a baby born at this gestation has."

I sighed. "I can't go to bed. Christa's only fifteen months old. And my job…"

"I'm telling you," he said sternly, "you could sneeze and have this baby!"

I nodded with a dumb face. I didn't know what I was going to do? What I did know was this baby I thought I didn't want had now become more precious to me than ever.

I needed Mom. She'd know what to do. Mother had started drawing her social security at age sixty-two and no longer worked.

*****

Catherine quickly responded to Diane's news over the phone. "Well, Honey, it's not going to be a problem. Rick can come and get me Monday mornings and I'll stay until Friday evenings. Then he can take me home for the weekends. He'll have Saturday and Sunday to take care of things and that'll give me a break."

"But, Mom, it's for three months."

"That's okay, Honey." Catherine couldn't think of anything she would rather do than care for her grandchildren while Diane rested in bed. It made her feel useful. She only wished someone didn't have to pick her up. But when her Mercury finally died, she didn't have money to buy another car.

That Monday, her new duties started, but they were nothing she hadn't done before. She cooked, cleaned, changed diapers, bathed kids, and did laundry.

For lunch on Tuesday, she made meatloaf. She prepared two plates and had just gotten Brian and Christa settled at the table when the phone rang. She picked up the receiver and cradled it between her shoulder and ear while she placed the pan back on the stove. "Hello," she said, a little short of breath.

"Well, hello." Hearing the familiar voice, she froze. "So you're there, huh?" Francis sounded calm, confident, and even friendly. She hadn't talked to him in almost seven years.

"Yes, I'm here." Why should she thrill at the sound of his voice? What was she thinking? It had almost killed her to know Diane and Rick had visited him and his new girlfriend, or wife or whatever, last Christmas. "You want to talk to Diane?"

"Yeah. But first, I want to talk to you."

Had she heard right? What could he have to say to her? "Oh?" Unless he loved her, there was nothing she wanted to hear.

"So tell me," he lowered his voice. "How's she really doing?" With his tone, one would have thought they were long lost friends confiding in one another, like nothing had ever happened between them.

"Well, I'm taking care of the children. She's resting, trying to not go into labor." She closed her eyes and in that moment her strength and resolve surfaced. She continued, but this time, devoid of emotion. "Every day she makes it, is that much better. Here, I'll let you talk to her." Without waiting for his response, she set the phone down and went to the bedroom.

"Your dad's on the phone. Why don't you pick up the extension?"

Returning, she silently hung up the phone. Catherine knew she'd never talk with him again, and that was okay. She'd been letting go ever since Diane said he'd married Ginny.

*****

Even though the doctor expected me to deliver any day, I had been praying, "Oh, Lord, please don't let this baby come before its due date." I was miserable and hurting all the time. It hurt to walk to the bathroom. On October 19th, 1979, her exact due date, April Michelle Yates was born. It was a grand day. I now not only had one perfect girl, but two. No brother for my perfect son, Brian, yet!

The years flew past. Rick and I served in our new church in Fort Worth. We taught Sunday school, ran a bus route on Sunday mornings, edited the church newsletter, and participated in Monday night visitation. God blessed our efforts and we saw many children make a decision to follow Christ. Mom visited our church on occasion, but didn't come faithfully.

Rick and I strived to visit Dad in California almost every year. He and Ginny lived vicariously and prospered in a nice house with a swimming pool, a gardener, and a maid who cleaned once a week. He owned more than one car lot and a boat. Dad belonged to the Yacht Club and played poker with Buddy Ebsen, aka Jed Clampitt, from *The Beverly Hillbillies*.

Once when we visited, I summoned the courage to talk with him about his faith.

"Dad, have you ever considered where you'll spend eternity?"

"I don't give it much thought. I don't think about that stuff." He quickly changed the subject. Dad didn't want any part of God.

Each time we visited, I could tell he wanted to impress me by his good fortune. Deep down, I was happy for him, but I kept my feelings inside. I couldn't forget the difficult times Mom and I had experienced.

It wasn't that I didn't think he should do well. I only wished Mother had nice things, too. He had discarded her, and me for that matter, like old shoes.

Chapter Twenty-One
1985

The clock struck eight. Diane and Rick would be here any minute. Catherine glanced at her black suit in the mirror. She clipped on her pearl earrings, ran a tube of lipstick over her lips, and grabbed her coat and Bible. She didn't want them to have to wait on her. She felt bad about them driving out of their way just to pick her up on Sunday morning.

Catherine watched out the window and saw the van drive up. Diane jumped out and slid open the van door. She was dressed in her royal blue dress with the belt tied tight around her slender waist and her long hair hanging in blonde spiral curls. Catherine locked the door on the way out.

"Hi, Mom. You look really nice." Diane helped her into the van.

"Oh, this old thing? I didn't think it looked too bad, though, for a seventy-two-year-old lady. Hi, Rick." She addressed her son-in-law.

"Now, Mom, you were our first stop," Diane explained while Rick maneuvered the van onto the freeway. "We still have four others."

"Well, Honey, I just feel so bad that you guys had to come get me."

"Don't be ridiculous."

Rick spoke up next. "We're driving the van anyway, picking up senior citizens who don't have another way to church. So you're our first stop."

"Well, you guys don't live as close since you moved. I hate for you to have to drive this far." Catherine wanted to go to church, but Rick and Diane bought a new house farther away from her. She didn't want to be an inconvenience.

"We're driving this far anyway, Mom." Diane smiled and patted her on the shoulder. "Besides, I don't want to drive a senior van route and not pick up my own mother!"

Catherine observed her grandchilddren, ages eleven, seven, and six, all dressed up with Bibles in hand. Diane and Rick talked as they drove along the freeway. She was proud of her daughter. Not only did Diane teach Sunday school, but she worked in other capacities at the church, all while raising three little children and running her own medical billing business.

As the years went by, Catherine continued to go to church with her daughter. God had spoken to her in many ways during the services. Though she had been away from Him, she realized He'd never left her. She could always rest in the loving hands of a big God.

When an apartment opened up only a mile from Diane, Catherine decided to move.

Linda, LouAnn, and Larry visited from time to time. She thanked God for her children. Audrey came for a visit each year. Buck flew her to Florida and took her to Disney World. Catherine found various ways to return to Missouri to see her siblings, whether with Diane or by bus.

Routinely, though, the days were long and lonely. She thought about the old times. She watched her soap operas. She'd cook things for different people in the apartment complex that might be sick. She cherished any time her grandchildren spent with her. Talking to her children on the phone always lifted her spirits. But, when there was nothing and no one else, she waited in anticipation for one of them to pay her a visit.

From her youth, she believed women were to marry, have children, and keep a home. She had worked hard to attain it. She had chased romance and love only to have it slip through her fingers. Having a nice home with modern conveniences, money as she need it, or even traveling the world all seemed distant and empty now. Her life, all of it, every single year, every suffering, every joy, were like vapors vanishing into time. Only yesterday, she had been young. Now in her old age, she struggled to comprehend life, struggled to understand all that really mattered.

In last Sunday's sermon, the pastor read *John 14:6*: "Jesus said I am the way, the truth and the life." She clung to that verse. In it she found hope, hope of a new life and a new eternal world with the one who truly loved her.

All this time she'd thought God was punishing her, but God works in mysterious ways. Would she ever have completely trusted in Him if she wasn't alone now? Diane had said she was better off without Francis. Maybe Diane was right. After all, with him gone, she spent her money the way she saw fit. She didn't have his socks to turn right side out, and laundry was a breeze. He didn't hog the TV and she could cook what she wanted.

*****

1992

With all the ingredients now in the bowl, Catherine stirred until they were completely mixed. Then she stood for a moment, staring at the bowl. As hard as she tried, she couldn't remember what she was making. She would leave it for a few minutes then maybe she'd remember.

Someone knocked on the door and she went to open it.

"Hi, Grandma," thirteen-year-old April stood on the doorstep, carrying a duffle bag.

"What do you got there, Honey?"

"It's my stuff. I've come to spend the night."

"You have?"

"Well, yeah! You called and I came. What's for dinner, Grandma?"

She didn't remember that April was coming over. "Well, good. I'm glad you came." She took April's face in her hands and kissed her cheek.

April went into the kitchen and looked at the bowl. "Oh, we're having meatloaf? Great, I like meatloaf."

"I knew that! That's why I made it." Now she remembered. Catherine poured the mixture into the loaf pan and placed it in the oven. She enjoyed the evening with April.

Catherine knew her mind failed her at times. She often found herself lost, even in her own apartment. Sometimes she didn't know what day it was. She needed to clean out her apartment and get her affairs in order.

Over the next few weeks, she methodically went through every box and souvenir, arranging them according to how she would disperse to each of her children and discarded what she didn't need. Carefully, she placed the new boxes in the closets. The pitcher Francis got her, the diamond ring Larry bought her, the jewelry sent to her by Linda and Audrey, the letters she wrote to

Kenneth, and letters from her mother, all little pieces of the history of her life.

*****

Around Easter, I spent the night with Mother in her apartment. It was out of the ordinary, but we went to sleep in her bed, just like the old days when I was a teenager. In the middle of the night, I felt Mother sit up. She probably had to go to the bathroom. But then, I heard a thud. I jumped up and turned on the light. Mother had fallen to the floor, hitting her head on the chest.

She appeared fine, but I knew otherwise. I talked with Linda and LouAnn and started taking Mother to various doctors, searching for answers. The last doctor, a neurologist, asked her a series of questions, which she couldn't remember. Her lack of memory shocked me! This was my mother, the woman who lived independently and always supported her children in their every endeavor.

The doctor suddenly ignored Mother as if she wasn't in the room, even though she sat right next to me. "She can no longer live by herself," he said. "It's not safe. She'll turn the stove on and forget to turn it off. She'll wander off and not remember where she is." His callousness stunned me. Why was he not talking to her?

I heard Mother take a deep breath. This neurologist couldn't have possibly been prepared for what happened next. Mother raised her voice with authority, lifting her head and staring him right in the eyes. "I live by myself. I pay my own bills, cook my own food, and do my own laundry—and I like it that way." She stood. "Come on Diane, we're leaving."

As I rose and nodded, a smirk crossed my lips. "Thank you, Doctor, but we're leaving." I couldn't have been prouder of her spunk.

As Mother progressively grew worse, Linda and I devised a plan where she could remain in her home as she desired. Linda would stay with her Monday through Wednesday. Then, from Thursday through Sunday, Mother would come to my house. We did this for a year, but then Linda's three-year-old grandson was diagnosed with Leukemia. Up until this time, Mother wouldn't even consider going to a nursing home, but when we told her about her great-grandson and how Linda needed to be there for him, she agreed. It was something she could do for Linda. The last decision Mom made was one of sacrifice. All of her children loved her for the sacrifices she had made over the years for each and every one of us.

I visited Mom in the nursing home often. When she first went there, I would pick her up and take her out. I didn't want her to feel confined. If I told her I would be there at four-thirty in the afternoon, she would be waiting for me at the entrance to the home, staring out the glass. But, as time passed and Mother could no longer leave, I would go and spend the whole day with her. She didn't really know me, but she knew I was somebody special. I would walk into her room and she'd smile. In the afternoon, we'd lie close together in her single bed and take a nap. I knew who she was, and that was all that mattered.

With Mother's condition, some patients become belligerent and combative, making them difficult to be around. Instead, Mother's spirit grew sweeter. All the nurses loved her and offered her the best of care.

One day when I went to see her, I brushed her hair and gave her a manicure. She didn't say a word. I observed her and considered all her worth. "Mom," I told her, "I think I'm going to write a book about you." Her eyes opened wider. "What do you think about that?" I asked.

She raised her eyebrows and pursed her lips as if to say, "Wouldn't that be something!"

Chapter Twenty-Two
1994

The sun set as Francis finished the work in his office. He got in his Cadillac and left his manager to close the lot. His frustration skyrocketed as he maneuvered through the road construction on Long Beach Boulevard, heading toward his apartment by the beach.

Ginny lived at their house in Lake Elsinore. They'd been together twenty years now, only lately, they weren't together. Her drinking had escalated out of control. She made a spectacle of them whenever they were in public. No matter how he pleaded with her to stop or even slow down, she wouldn't listen. It was just easier for him to move into an apartment and not drive the seventy miles a day to and from work only to be subjected to her.

A flagman turned the slow sign to stop and Francis slammed on the brakes. He hit the steering wheel with his fist. "Oh, my god! Are they ever going to get finished with this stupid trolley line? It's killing my business." He pushed the lighter in and put a cigarette in his mouth. The city had decided to lay the trolley rails down Long Beach Boulevard, passing right in front of his car lot. He cursed this dreadful project that threatened his business. "I can't believe this. I've lost money now nine months in a row. Nine months!" The city had said it would be completed months ago. He turned onto Redondo Boulevard and stopped at another light.

Francis grew agitated when he stopped at his fifth red light. He watched pedestrians cross the street, mostly younger people with all of life in front of them. They laughed and appeared happy. The light turned green and he pushed down on the accelerator. Sharp pain shot down his arm. His chest felt tight and heavy. He tried to inhale, but couldn't catch his breath. No, he couldn't have a heart attack right now. He didn't have time for it. The car moved along at thirty miles an hour. Breathing became almost impossible as the pain increased.

Francis made a left turn at the next intersection. He could see St. Mary Medical Center. An ambulance, siren blaring, pulled into the circle drive in front of him. Following the signs for the emergency entrance, he parked. He managed to walk through the automatic door and sign the register.

A young nurse in scrubs came around the counter. "Mr. Burch, what's going on this evening?"

He took as deep a breath as possible. "I can't get my breath and my chest hurts."

She snapped her fingers. "I need a wheelchair here, stat." No sooner had she finished demanding than it arrived. Francis fell into it. The next thing he knew, he was in a room with nurses buzzing around him. After drawing blood and performing an EKG, they started an IV and placed an oxygen tube in his nose. The doctor examined him and ordered a barrage of tests.

Sometime later, Dr. Gupta entered again with his clipboard. "So Mr. Burch, you *have* had a heart attack."

Francis raised his brows, "Oh, so it was a heart attack?"

"Yes, but you got here in good time. I think we should admit you to the cardiac floor. Then tomorrow we need to do a heart cath." Francis struggled to understand Dr. Gupta's accent.

"Well, okay."

"How many years you've smoked?"

"Since I was fifteen." The doctor nodded, but didn't say anymore.

The next day, after the heart cath and return of the test results, the doctor entered his room.

"Mr. Burch, the good news is we were able to place stents in your blocked arteries. In the old days, we would've had to do bypass surgery."

Up until this point, Francis had never really been sick. "What's the bad news?" he asked.

Dr. Gupta sat the chart down and looked directly at him. "I'm afraid you have advanced lung disease, Emphysema, COPD. We'll start some meds for your heart and I've ordered breathing treatments. We'll see how you do with that."

Francis nodded. "Okay."

Dr. Gupta continued. "Your smoking, it has affected your lungs and deprived the heart of oxygen. Mr. Burch, you need to stop smoking."

Francis nodded, but thought to himself, *There's no way I'm going to stop smoking.*

He was in the hospital for two weeks and not able to go to work for another two. By the time he returned, his business was on the edge of collapse. Trying to salvage what he could, he sold his boat and closed the second lot. He reduced staff, but at the age of sixty-eight, his body waned, unable to work like before. Francis once again cursed the closing of Long Beach Boulevard and his failing health. He had been on top of the world, successful and affluent. Now, his world was crumbling around him.

He and Ginny had officially called it quits. One day, he met Lydia, who was from the Philippines and a good fifteen years younger. He liked her, but something in his life was missing, a void he couldn't fill.

On Sunday afternoon, he picked up the phone and dialed the numbers, anxious to hear a loving voice.

"Hello," Diane answered.

"Yeah, what's going on?"

*****

After Dad's heart attack, I knew he'd been struggling. He complained to me more than once about the road construction and how it had hurt his business.

"Same ole, same ole," I responded. "What about you? How are you doing?"

"I don't know what I'm going to do." He sounded desperate.

"Well, Dad, maybe you should let the business go. Just close and cut your losses."

"If I do that, I'll never work again."

"You know, Dad, having money and things isn't really what's important."

"I don't know about that. If it isn't money, what is it?"

I thought carefully about the words I wanted to use, trying to put myself in his head. "You're sixty-eight. When you look back at all that time, doesn't it seem like it was over in the snap of your fingers? When it's really over, what's all that matters?" He didn't say anything so I continued. "Being close to the ones you love. Spending time with them."

He was quiet. I wanted to say, "How's your relationship with God, Dad?" But I didn't think the time was right.

He broke the silence. "So how are *you* doing?"

Had I heard right? He actually asked about me! "Oh, it's just crazy around here." Tears filled my eyes. "I'm losing Mom. She's dying and it's hard, you know."

"She *is* dying? They've said that?"

"Well, she has Alzheimer's. It's inevitable." We talked a little more before saying goodbye.

*****

About four weeks later, Dad called again. "Well, Gizmo, I'm ready. I closed the lot. I just need you to come out here and help me pack up my stuff." I couldn't have been more shocked, but Rick and I both felt God could be in this. I flew to California and helped him pack his apartment. We shipped boxes and boarded a plane for home.

Dad rented an apartment not too far from me and less than a mile from the nursing home where Mother resided. I helped him get settled. When darkness fell and I got in my car to leave, I glanced at his window. He was standing there, waving goodbye. It reminded me of when my children were small and waved goodbye when I left for work.

Brian now lived in California with roommates and attended college. Christa and

April were both in high school and rebellious. My business required much of my attention, but with what little time I had left over, I visited Dad and squeezed in visits to see Mom. Life pulled me in so many different directions that I almost lost my way.

One day when I visited Dad, he mentioned, "You know, I'd really like to go to Mountain Grove." He wanted to visit his cousin and her husband.

He took a drink of his coffee. "You know I had another cousin, Vinita. She's gone, but her daughter, Doris, married Frankie McCune. I think he's a preacher. You probably don't remember them."

"I know Frankie and Doris." I answered him while my mind explored trip possibilities.

Dad continued. "Vinita's old man, Melvin, is still alive. I'd like to see him again, too."

Most of the other relatives were gone, but I wanted to return to the place my grandparents had lived, also. I could use a vacation and a break from all the stress.

"Well, let's go." I think I startled him. "Just the two of us. We'll go up through Arkansas and make a trip of it." It was a good idea and an opportunity for Dad and me to maybe grow a little closer. This was a chance to spend time with him and to show my love for him, something Jesus would do.

"Okay, let's do it."

We set out early Friday morning. We drove through Little Rock and turned north. We spent the night in Mountain Home, Arkansas. We ate at a little diner across from the town square and noticed musicians gathering on the lawn with all kinds of stringed instruments. We listened to them play bluegrass tunes until late. Dad was like a kid in a candy store! I enjoyed watching him.

The next day, as we continued driving through the Ozark Mountains, Dad pointed out all the beauty surrounding us: the scenic views, the rushing waters, the mountains of rich soil, and the beautiful trees. I realized we enjoyed the same things. I never once suspected I had inherited my love of nature from my dad!

Mom felt the soil beneath her feet and imagined the crops it could yield or the pasture it afforded, but Dad saw the beauty in the flowers and the rolling hills. She recognized the lush, green trees of spring for the shade they provided in the summer or the fruit and nuts they produced in the fall, where Dad enjoyed the splendor of their foliage. She knew winter always lurked around the corner, leaving barren branches laden with ice and snow in the bitter cold. Mom saw clear flowing water providing buckets for cool drinks, cooking, laundry, and cleaning.

As I drove, Dad operated the cassette player. We listened mostly to Bob Wills and the sound of "Ah, hah" as he sang songs like "San Antonio Rose," "Steel Guitar Rag," and "Stay a Little Longer." I knew I was making precious memories.

"Hey, Diane! Turn here and let's go to Hodgson's Mill."

"Do you know how to get there?"

"I bet I could get there in my sleep."

"Then I'm game. I love doing things like this."

I followed the winding gravel road up and down hills, taking it slow. Weeds and brush crowded on both sides. Trees surrounded us. I parked the car outside the long ago closed structure. The water fell over the cliff side and flowed down by the mill. It was beautiful and such a shame it was closed. We walked around and drank from the cool fresh water.

I could tell Dad was lost in time, perhaps in a time of steam-powered trains and one-room schoolhouses, a time without trucks and traffic, before jet airliners flew the skies.

*****

Francis glanced at Diane as she drove. He'd enjoyed this trip and spending time with his daughter. He soaked in the sights of the Ozarks, his homeland, as the car meandered along the highway. When he wasn't talking, he was thinking, remembering. He missed his folks. He wished his mind would stop playing this old hymn. It just kept going over and over. It started last night when he laid down in the motel room and tried to sleep.

Precious mem'ries, how they linger, how they ever flood my soul

In the stillness of the midnight, precious, sacred scenes unfold.

I remember mother praying, Father, too, on bended knee

Sun is sinking, shadows falling, but their pray'rs still follow me.

J.B.F. Wright, 1925

As his breaths became labored, Francis pulled his inhaler out of his pocket. If it wasn't for that inhaler, he didn't know what he'd do. His dad had died at the age of seventy-two. Francis was sixty-eight. How long would he live? He had no control over it. His hands shook at the thought.

*****

September 1995

Francis found himself California dreamin' again. This last year in Texas had been good, but now the western sun beckoned him. He wanted to return to the land of dreams. After he taped the last box, he decided to take a drive before packing his suitcase. Lydia was going to meet him at the airport tonight.

He drove down Belknap Street and turned right onto Baker Boulevard. He could see Richland Hills Nursing Home down Kings Court. This was where Catherine lived. He drew a deep breath. Diane had asked him not to go there, and all this time he'd honored her request. This morning, however, a strong magnetic force drew him. He found himself turning right on Kings Court. His heart pounded as he parked the car on the street and walked toward the door. He proceeded down the hallway. As he approached her room, he suddenly stopped. He almost turned around. Involuntarily, his body continued, his feet moving as if they had a mind of their own and crossing the threshold of her door.

She sat quietly in the chair beside her bed, a high chair of sorts with the tray across the front. She was petite and fragile, her gray hair curled and soft. She lifted her head and saw him. Instantly, she smiled and her lips parted slightly, as if she knew him. Her eyes sparkled and tears formed in his. A wheelchair folded in the corner of the room caught his attention. He was reminded of a promise he'd made years ago. How much the two of them had changed since those days when they were happy together!

He stood there willing his mouth to open, willing the words "I'm sorry" to come out, but they wouldn't. The words were stuck somewhere in the back of his throat. His hands shook, and he was lost.

He turned and walked away. So lost was he, his soul might never find its way.

Chapter Twenty-Three
November 2000

The Bradford pear tree in our front yard turned brilliant red. I loved the fall in my Missouri home. Rick and I moved here two years ago. The little town of Fayette possessed one flashing light, and two cars posed a traffic jam! The courthouse stood in the middle of the town square, and the gazebo on its lawn hosted brass bands. Every Fourth of July, the whole countryside came together for fireworks and picnics.

After raising three children and enduring the hustle and bustle of the Dallas/Fort Worth rat race, God led us here to Fayette, Missouri. I thought about the 23rd *Psalm* I memorized as a child, "He leads me beside the still water, He restores my soul."

The phone rang and I hurried to answer it. "Hello."

"Yeah, what's going on?" I heard Dad's voice at the other end.

I asked him how he was doing. I knew he'd had another heart attack, requiring more stents. The doctors finally got him to stop smoking, but he was already suffering from end stage lung disease. To make matters worse, he'd just gotten over several months of a severe case of shingles. His legs hurt and his back hurt so much he had to have shots in his spine. He asked me if we liked it in Fayette.

"Maybe I'll move there," he said.

"Well, I think you'd like it." How many times had Dad moved in his life, only to become restless and want to move again? "But, Dad, if you move here and don't like it, I don't want you complaining. Rick and I are happy here."

"I just want to live someplace where it's close to drive to the store," he explained. "Somewhere I can maybe meet some people over coffee. Drive to church on Sundays."

I did a double blink. Did I hear correctly? Dad said he's going to drive to church? Hearing those words coming from him sounded foreign. "Well, that fits Fayette to a T."

Lydia drove Dad from sunny California to Missouri at the end of November. He rented a house not far from mine. That December and January, we experienced heavy snowfall, and I'm sure he started to rethink his decision.

*****

Francis's own body, plagued by disease and ailments, made his life miserable. He gave himself breathing treatments three times a day. He couldn't sleep at night or sit in the day because of pain in his legs.

Every night, he was afraid to go to sleep for fear he might not wake up. What was there after this life? His parents believed in heaven. They believed in a savior, but he'd always rejected him. He had never wanted that lifestyle. He'd been taught Christ died for his sins, but how could someone like him ever be close to God? He didn't know what to do or how to prepare to die. Diane and his sister, Lois, had talked with him about accepting Christ. He'd even told them he wanted to, but then he still resisted.

He needed to go to Mountain Grove and see Frankie McCune. As the pastor of a church, maybe Frankie could guide him. Frankie was a musician, so they shared a common bond. Frankie had always accepted him for who he was and never made him feel like he wasn't good enough.

Diane drove him down there. The sun shone outside as the four of them, Doris, Diane, Frankie, and him, sat in the Mc-Cune's living room.

Diane and Doris were talking when Frankie asked him, "Francis, you want to go outside and talk?"

"Yeah, let's do that." Even though he agreed, Francis immediately started shaking. What was he going to say? What would Frankie think? Maybe he couldn't do this after all.

The two of them walked to some old metal lawn chairs underneath a tree. Francis sat in one and Frankie pulled the other around. Facing him, Frankie leaned forward.

"Francis, I feel there's something you need to talk about." He paused for a moment. "Have you been thinking about eternity lately?"

"Maybe." How did Frankie know what he'd been thinking?

"Well, you know Jesus died for *you*. He already did it, Brother, it's done. All you have to do is ask Him to be your savior."

Francis's hands started trembling again. "Not sure I can." He wanted to, but pride stood in his way.

"Well, it's something only you can do. A choice you have to make. I can't do it for you. God loves us and wants us to choose Him. Jesus said, 'I am the way, the truth, and the life. No man comes to the father except by me.'"

This was a hard thing for Francis. "I've made a lot of mistakes." He stared at the ground for a moment. "I don't think he'll want me."

Frankie placed a hand on his shoulder. "You're a sinner just like me, Brother. All you have to do is ask Him. Is that something you want to do? Something you're ready to do?"

He hesitated, but then nodded. "I think…I am."

There, in Frankie's backyard, in the land of his birth, he bowed his head and allowed a man of God to lead him to his Savior. He wondered if those in heaven knew.

*****

Fayette was a small town. Several churches, the grocery store, the pharmacy, and even Francis's primary care doctor were all conveniently located near the square. Only doctor appointments with a specialist required him to drive to a larger city.

The senior center served good lunches and a chance to meet others. Francis played cards, shot some pool, and made many friends. He attended various churches and found himself most at home sitting in a pew, listening to a preacher.

Whenever he drew his last breath, which could be any day, and came face-to-face with the Almighty, he wondered if God would be pleased with him, knowing he'd lived his whole life only for himself. Certainly, God wouldn't say, "Well done, thy good and faithful servant."

Guilt tormented his sleep, causing Francis to doubt the faith he'd only recently found. There must be something more he should do, some price he should pay for his past. He found himself pacing the floor at night, once again afraid to sleep.

Even though he did everything within his power to be with people, he couldn't escape the loneliness of his own house. Without playing the TV or the radio all the time, the silence of the four walls was deafening.

*****

2002

The phone rang, rousing me from a coveted night of sleep. Rick looked at the caller ID. "It's your dad," he announced before answering, "Hello."

I looked at the clock and saw it was two in the morning. *Is Dad having a heart attack? Has something awful happened?* After a few seconds, Rick said, "Frank, it's two in the morning!" He placed his hand over the speaker and turned to me. "He wants to know if you can put Tupperware in the microwave!"

My jaw dropped. I blinked and nodded. "Tell him yes." Why would Dad wake us up when he knew we had to work that day?

When Rick hung up, I asked, "What did he say when you told him what time it was?"

"He said he knew, but he needed to know if you could put Tupperware in the microwave!"

I shook my head. This wasn't the first time Dad had called in the middle of the night. Many times I had taken him to the ER for symptoms appearing to be a heart attack caused by anxiety.

*****

September 2004

Dad struggled with severe anemia. The doctor sent him to the hospital to receive a blood transfusion. While there, the urologist talked him into having surgery on his prostate. One complication after another required him to remain in the hospital for two months, first in ICU, then a regular room, finally a skilled nursing floor. During this time, his strength diminished and full recovery appeared doubtful.

"Hi, Dad," I said as I entered his room. Since I worked across the street from the hospital, I'd go over and eat lunch with him. This being a big election year, we watched news coverage on the campaign. After work, I would go visit him again for an hour or two before driving my forty-five-minute commute home. No matter how late I stayed, he never wanted me to leave.

Upon his eventual discharge from the hospital, he required a wheelchair, a permanent suprapubic catheter, and admission to Fayette Caring Center.

Just like with Mom, I didn't want Dad to feel confined. Whenever he felt like it, I would pick him up and we'd go driving around. Sometimes, when the weather was pretty, we would drive around on a golf cart.

As time lapsed, he only grew weaker and the hope of complete recovery evaporated.

*****

Francis hated the nursing home. He hated the bland, mushy food. He hated the screaming. Sometimes, he even hated the nurses.

Down the hall and in the great room, he found the only highlight in a day: the electric organ, which he would play whenever he got the chance. A lady, who'd recently become a resident, also played. Occasionally, a church group visited and played songs. He lived for those times. Most of the residents couldn't really communicate, but he wasted no time in identifying the few that could. He'd push the wheels of his chair and make the rounds daily to check on them.

Francis's body failed him, but his mind remained sharp. He wondered which was worse: losing your mind, or losing the use of your body.

The evening sun set and Reji, a black nurse, entered his room to empty his catheter bag. "It's about dinner time, Mr. Burch. You want me to wheel you down to the dining room?" he asked.

"Not tonight." Francis was excited. "My daughter's bringing me prime rib."

Reji flushed the toilet and returned. "Wow! How do you rate that?"

He chuckled. "She gets it every Thursday night before she leaves Columbia. It's from the Outback Steakhouse, their

Thursday night special." He started clearing off his tray while talking.

"She must really love you, huh?" Reji hooked the bag back on the wheelchair.

Francis shrugged. "I guess."

The last thing on the tray Francis removed was a belt buckle, a present from Pastor Dale, who'd painted a beautiful design on it himself. Francis ran his fingers over its smooth finish. He could feel the love in that gift.

Dale pastored the First Baptist Church of Fayette and came often to visit him. Why, even two days ago, Dale bought him a new pair of pants. Most of the clothes hanging in Francis's closet didn't fit because of all the weight he lost in the hospital.

Francis had talked to Pastor Dale about being baptized, thinking maybe eventually he'd feel like going to church and climbing the steps into the baptistery. Now, he doubted he'd ever be able to do that. Still, he wanted to be baptized.

Francis watched the door and heard footsteps coming down the hall. Could it be Diane's heels approaching his room? The sound of plastic bags rubbing against each other confirmed it.

"Hi, Dad." She walked in still dressed from work.

His spirits lifted immediately. "What took you so long?"

"Outback had a line." She started taking containers out of the bags.

"It smells good." His mouth watered.

Diane placed his silverware next to his plate. "Well, why don't I pray and we'll get started before it gets colder," she said.

He remembered a time when he despised those who insisted on praying before eating. Now, he actually bowed his head, closed his eyes, and paid reverence to God. His grandfather, who had been a professor of law in Dublin, immigrated to the States before the turn of the century. Francis remembered him saying in his rogue Irish accent, "God 'n be damned, do ye think it went any higher than the ceiling?" Now, if only his grandfather were here, he'd tell him, "Yes, Grandpa, I do."

"This prime rib certainly puts the mush in the dining room to shame!" he told his daughter.

"I got two loaves of bread. I really love their bread." The two of them briefly stopped talking and enjoyed their food.

"I talked to Pastor Dale," Francis told her. "He said he's been thinking about a way I can be baptized."

"Really? How's he going to get you to church?"

"He says he thinks he can do it here."

"Oh?"

"Yeah, I hope he can. I'd sure like to be baptized."

Diane smiled. "I know you would, Dad."

They finished eating. "Do you want me to help you stand for a little bit?" she asked.

Sitting in the wheelchair all day made his hips, legs, and back hurt. Standing always felt good. He was too weak to stand on his own, but she could help stabilize and support him. They stood for several minutes, facing each other.

As his eyes met hers, there was so much he wanted to tell his little girl. He'd had a lot of time to think about his life and all the mistakes he'd made. If he could live life over again, things would be different, but there were no do overs. Francis opened his mouth and looked into her eyes. It was now or never.

"You know, I didn't always do right," he ventured. "I just want to say," he drew a deep breath. "I'm sorry about the past," There, he said it.

She shook her head, "Oh, Dad, don't worry about the past. We live for now and the future."

Francis was finally beginning to realize what really mattered. Money, cars, nice houses, boats, prestige, and country clubs seemed of little significance now. What really mattered was living the way

Jesus wanted. Unfortunately, he'd already lived and there was precious little he could do now.

He needed to say more, his head level with hers, their faces only inches apart. "You know, I've made a lot of money in my life. And I'm ashamed of how I've spent it."

Diane smiled and nodded. "But, Dad, Jesus forgave all that when you turned to Him."

Francis felt tired and needed to sit again.

*****

July 30, 2005

It was Saturday. I went to visit Dad, saw his coloring, and immediately knew something was wrong. The charge nurse examined him and offered to call his doctor, but I insisted we call an ambulance and take him to the hospital.

As we waited for the ambulance, to our surprise, Frankie McCune walked into his room. He had driven three hours from Mountain Grove to see Dad. "I woke up early and felt like God wanted me to come," he explained. Frankie brought his guitar and played some hymns Dad wanted to hear.

The ambulance arrived and we all left for Columbia and Boone Hospital. Even though I was concerned, I fully expected Dad to be treated and released.

In the ER, Frankie prayed with Dad and played his guitar some more, comforting a sinner saved by grace. Tears filled my eyes when the alarms on the monitors went off and medical staff ushered me out of the room as they worked on him. They brought him back to join me again for twenty-three more hours, but on Sunday, July 31st, 2005, Jesus carried Dad to his new home.

Chapter Twenty-Four

Life is not always a happy-ever-after. But then our hope is not in this life; we're all only passing through. The kingdom of Heaven is at hand.

On a cold January day in 1997, with ice on the roads in Fort Worth, Texas, Mother finally reached the end of her earthly journey. She was home as she had said in my dream, "Here in the mountains."

Her family celebrated her in a little chapel as the pastor preached about the woman who served her family in *Proverbs 31*. That chapter said, "Strength and honor are her clothing, and she shall rejoice in time to come." We each shared about a special time Mom touched our lives. Two of her grandchildren, Al and Christa, sang "Amazing Grace," a song dear to her heart. I and my siblings rose up and called her blessed for her resourcefulness, sacrifice, and care.

Mom was laid to rest in a beautiful cemetery she had chosen, not far from where she had spent her last years. Regardless, she is not there. She lives surrounded in a beauty unsurpassed by anything we know here, safe in the arms of a Savior who always loved her and never left her.

Eight years later, my husband, children, and I, along with family and friends, gathered to reflect upon Francis Burch, who had lived his life and done it his way. He was a father, brother, uncle, grandfather, and great-grandfather. We all rejoiced that he, at seventy-five years of age, had asked Jesus to save him before entering eternity. His granddaughter, Christa, endeavored to sing "Amazing Grace," but only made it through the first verse. Frankie finished it for her.

Dad was laid to rest beside his folks in the cemetery of his parents' country church, not two miles from where he had taken Mother for a romantic picnic beside a gentle flowing stream. I live today because their lives crossed years ago and they comforted one another.

Francis's life had taken him on many journeys, some exciting, others difficult, but God was faithful to all those who had prayed for him. Like the changed thief hanging on the cross beside Jesus, unworthy and drowning in sin, Francis lives today in Paradise.

He and Catherine are whole and clothed in the righteousness of the Savior, whose saving grace is *all that matters.*

Afterword

I'm thankful for my mom and dad. I'm thankful for the hard times we had as well as the good ones. God used those times to sculpt and inspire who I am today. Each struggle or joy prepared me for my life's path. As I look back, I can see His mighty hand at work molding, guiding, and changing me.

56515083R00179

Made in the USA
Charleston, SC
20 May 2016